MW00531781

In One Ear and Out the Other

Essential guide for effective communication

In One Ear and Out the Other

Essential guide for effective communication

Robert J. Rubel, PhD
Veronica M. Petterson

RED EIGHT BALL PRESS
AUSTIN

Red Eight Ball Press

PO box 171303, Austin, TX 78717

In One Ear and Out the Other:

Essential guide for effective communication

© 2020 Robert J. Rubel and Veronica M. Petterson

All rights reserved. No part of this work may be reproduced or utilized in any form or by any means, electronic or mechanical, including photocopying, micro-film, and recording, or by any information storage and retrieval system, without permission in writing from the authors or the publisher. All quoted material is either used with the permission of the authors, is in the public domain, or can be considered "fair use" under copyright law.

Edited by Patrick Califia

Cover art by Robert J. Rubel and Veronica Petterson

Layout design by kitara

Printed in the United States of America

ISBN 978-0-9968795-6-9

LCCN 2020904880

To those of you who have the courage to seek resources to help you to strengthen your communication skills. Congratulations! This is a path for those who understand they must work on themselves in order to improve the way they interact with others. This is a book about taking personal responsibility for your communication. Communication is the key to building great relationships that thrive. In solid relationships, everyone feels heard, validated, and understood. This is true whether in the workplace, in social settings, or at home.

We hope this book adds effective tools to your relationship toolbox.

Foreword

Why a book on communications? Excellent question. Bob and I write, teach, and conduct workshops internationally about relationship issues. More than anything else, we find that relationship conflict is rooted in communication glitches. One person says *boulder* and the other interprets it *landslide*.

Oddly, we engage in five major aspects of adult life without much (or any) formal training. These are areas we bumble though, hoping for the best:

- Communication

- Sex

- Relationships

- Finances

- Parenting

For some reason, our culture seems to believe that we will just learn how to become successful with practice or through osmosis. Generally, we aren't taught these skills in school, and once we are adults, we're on our own.

We have all had arguments, right? Do you get better at arguing based upon how often you argue? We tend to listen to respond rather than listen to understand. We may be so busy composing a rebuttal that we miss the vulnerable truth in the other person's speech. That's our first gem for you. However, it takes work to make that gem sparkle. Take the time to learn to listen with empathy and caring. It is the first step in being a good listener.

Are you ready to become a more effective communicator? The first step is learning how to listen. While many books are written about how to get your point across, communication is actually like a two-way street filled with loud and speedy traffic, barriers and blockades. Imagine yourself on one side of that street and the person with whom you are trying to communicate is on the other side. Neither of you can cross, and you are trying to get messages to each other. All those barriers (figurative cars driving by, loud mufflers, horns honking, etc.) are your personal perspectives and filters that stand in the way of actually hearing what someone is saying to you. How do we get from this noisy, busy street to better understanding?

Strap on your seatbelt. This book provides communication strategies and approaches you can use in your daily life to help you navigate that perilous, noisy street to stand quietly next to someone and communicate effectively.

This book is designed to bring up key topics in a general way. You can start using this information immediately. You'll have areas to explore more deeply on your journey to become a better communicator.

—Veronica Petterson

Note

Works mentioned in this book are formally listed chapter by chapter in the "Cited Works" section of the *Supplementary Material*. This avoids breaking the flow of ideas by inserting citations in the body of the book.

In some cases (particularly quotes commonly found in collections of clever phrases), we provide the name of the person who is attributed with having spoken those words, but we have no way of tracing such quotes to original sources.

Contents

ON RELATIONSHIP AS VOCATION

People pursue many careers, many passions—many do so
without any specific plan while others pursue them
with a concerted effort. Diligence. Strategy. Goals.
What if we sought relationships with such dedication?

Imagine creating a résumé for a relationship position, listing
all of the skills and experiences that might qualify you for
the position you hope to secure. Attributes. Experience.
Training. References. Contact information.

Imagine applying for a relationship for the purpose of learning
what duties would be expected and how it would be rewarded.
Imagine the interview process—what would you say?
How would you offer yourself to another?

Imagine having a relationship based on this understanding,
one with clear expectations and requirements, one which
would continue as long as the criteria were met, or be
terminated if one's performance was unsatisfactory?

We seek meaning in our lives. We seek expression.
We seek gainful employment and a place to live.
We seek nourishment and enjoyable experiences.
What if relationships embodied what we seek?

—Gem

Chapter 1

Getting on the same page

> "A man is known by the company his mind keeps."
>
> —Thomas Bailey Aldrich

HAVE YOU PLAYED THE game telephone? You sit as a group in a circle. One person starts by whispering a phrase to the person next to them. That person then whispers what they think they heard to the person next to them, and so on and so forth until the phrase makes it to the person sitting on the other side of the initiator. That person announces out loud what they heard.

The initiator now reveals the phrase that began the game. Invariably, the message has become mangled as it's whispered all the way 'round. By the end, it's unimaginably and hilariously distorted from the original. Often, when we hear something and it goes through all of our various filters, it is actually a garbled, barely recognizable caricature of the sender's original message.

Many/most communication glitches result from differences in languaging skills, background, and life experiences. Someone says something (anything) and it is slightly misinterpreted by the listener. Suddenly, the discussion is *slightly* off track, but neither party recognizes this at first. It may take some time to realize there is a widening schism between what was meant and what was heard, if it is noticed at all. It can be difficult to figure out where the first misunderstanding happened when one person has stormed off (or shut down emotionally) and the other is confused by this bizarre turn of events.

Lose/lose.

Because of this, we have included quite a bit of material about techniques for listening to understand, removing communication filters, de-escalating upsets, and methods for teasing apart communication blocks, as well as how to apologize in such a way that you can begin to heal any rifts that might occur.

If you are in a relationship, chances are both parties want it to work. There is a built-in give-and-take when speaking together. In the best of worlds, you and your partner are reading this book together and your improved speaking and listening skills will pay off with mutual benefits. However, we sometimes have partners whose vision differs from ours and you're reading this book on your own.

This is not a bad thing, for it is similar to workplaces. At work, you must interact with people with various backgrounds and communication skills. For that reason, we provide ample tips, techniques, and strategies for improving communication with someone who might not be as invested (or motivated) to seek a positive outcome.

Orientation

In order for two people to meet, they must communicate. Upon meeting and getting past culture-bound pleasantries (but before saying anything that signals actual interest in getting to know the person), people automatically run through strategies for saying something—*anything*. However, in our experience, what you first say is less important than your first response. Convey that you understood what they said and considered it when replying. As Stephen R. Covey noted in his book *The 7 Habits of Highly Effective People: Powerful Lessons in Personal Change*: "Most people do not listen with the intent to understand; they listen with the intent to reply."

Words are the most powerful force available to humanity. We can choose to use this force constructively with words of encouragement, or destructively with words of dismissal. Words have energy and power. They have the ability to bond people to you or drive them away. As Yehuda Berg has observed, words can be used "to help, to heal, to hinder, to hurt, to harm, to humiliate and to humble." More than that, words often have multiple meanings; there can be second- and third-level connotations. That's what makes language so expressive; it is also what makes clear speaking such a challenge.

People need to be recognized as individuals; they also need to feel heard and acknowledged. If you can provide that level of validation with your initial exchanges, you will make a profound impression. To the extent that you can authentically create a feeling of rapport with people, you will make friends who will stay with you your entire life.

To communicate effectively, it helps to recognize that people see the world through their own (highly individualized) perspectives. You will gain a communication advantage when you use this understanding to guide and improve your discussions with others.

You are not born with the ability to communicate clearly. You were not even brought up to see the world objectively. Commonly, you stumble through conversations by translating what you hear someone say, filtered through your own perspectives about how life works.

Fortunately, you can learn a wide range of communication techniques. It's not rocket science. You can improve communication with someone by discovering how they solve problems and manage information. However, much like any skill, you have to commit yourself to working at it. If you accept this challenge, you will quickly start to see improvements in your daily interactions.

Once your communications toolbox contains an array of techniques, you will be able to match the appropriate techniques to the particular challenge. However, this takes practice. Practicing communication skills is much like practicing how to disassemble a bomb: The more the better.

The variables that affect the way we perceive and respond to someone else are exceedingly complex. When listening to someone, their words flow through our unconscious thought/logic processes and experience-based filters. Examples include our upbringing, socioeconomic status, education level, personality type, prejudices, and learning styles. Actually, there is a dizzying array of additional factors (such as cultural traditions) that slant and skew our perspectives in ways that govern how we behave in every interaction. The net effect is that we may not say exactly what we mean because we are speaking in our own code. Obviously, the person with whom we're speaking is listening to our words with their own filters and prejudices. Clear communication is a challenging project.

Communication miscues can be very subtle and build precariously over time. When one person has based their behavior on what turns out to be misinterpretations of the other person's reality, a seemingly calm and polite conversation can change to a *fight-or-flight* situation when no one ever intended that outcome. Later in this book, we will show you a number of techniques to identify, redirect, and defuse volatile interactions.

By the way, we like to write in the first-person present tense, as though we're speaking directly to you. Just consider this book to be a personal visit. In addition, we write and present in spirals. Often, we will introduce a topic lightly at first, then bring it in again with a little more detail, and discuss it in more depth a third time. We do this in order to build up your knowledge around that topic. By the time you're exposed to the detailed discussion, the ideas sound familiar.

Concepts to consider

Russell Hoban once observed: "When you come right down to it, how many people speak the same language even when they speak the same language?" (*A Russell Hoban Omnibus*). When I (Bob) first read that sentence many decades ago, I wondered... *Why is that so?* However, the older I grew, the more sense it made.

For most of us, the way we speak and listen has developed from survival reactions that began at our birth. Your parent(s) raised their voice(s) and you made that mean something. Perhaps they told you forcibly to be quiet, and you—not understanding they were stressed about something else—reacted in your own inexperienced world as though *you* had done something wrong.

Human instinct taught you to build defenses. You may have learned to become more assertive or you may have learned to become more passive. Perhaps your parents exhibited other types of dysfunctional communication, such as being passive-aggressive, evasive, sarcastic, etc. Or perhaps they excelled at good and clear communication but you, yourself, built walls that stand in your way to this day.

Regardless, over the years, your upbringing and early adult experiences played a dominant role in shaping the personality you now have.

Unless you have studied communication techniques (and worked consciously to alter the way you listen to others and react to what they say), chances are that your current communication style is fundamentally the same as it was when you were 15 or so. Basically, this means that your early social conditioning is still with you. For example, the way you react to authority figures probably developed from the way you were permitted to react to your own parents' authority.

It's all about your choices

We share three beliefs that permeate this book:

1   **What you see is what you get**. If you are focusing on (and seeking) positives, you will get feedback that is positive. On the negative side of the equation, you get what you resist—because you focus on it. So, when we exert the time and energy to foster good communication, our work and personal relationships tend to improve.

2   **Sustainable relationships are not accidental.** Relationships worth having require work. You choose whether or not to be a good partner on a moment-by-moment basis. Will you choose to phone it in or actively work toward making it as enriching and rewarding as you want it to be?

3   **"If it's going to be, it's up to me."** Recurring patterns can be changed. Only you are in charge of you. Your past doesn't have to be your future. Who will you choose to be? The ball is in your court.

These distinctions are important, as this book is meant to help you draw attention to your personal responsibility in communication. The purpose in examining the way you speak is to figure out what works (and hang onto those), figure out what is actually unhelpful (and unlearn them), and discover new skill sets to help you on your path to clearer communication. In the same sense that our upbringing, education, and life experiences influence who we perceive ourselves to be, *who we perceive ourselves to be* colors our relationships. Our relationships influence our self-image, including the ways we walk, interact with others, and dress in everyday life. Critically, our self-image affects our professional success.

Knowing yourself and your communication partner(s)

Let's start with *willingness*. Communication is a two-way street. At least one person has to transmit information and at least one person must be **willing** to receive that information. Bob and I repeatedly say this in our communication and relationships presentations: "It [communication and relationships] is only as important as the least interested party." If the person with whom you are attempting to communicate is unwilling or unable to receive and understand that information, you can go no further. Make sure that you both agree that understanding and mutually beneficial resolutions are the end goals **before** the conversation begins.

Under optimal conditions, you and your partner(s) are working through this book together. However, this book isn't about perfect conditions. Your interactions will improve a great deal even if you are the only one working on better communication. Effective communication reduces misunderstandings. It removes as many filters as possible, allowing you to transmit and receive clear messages without emotional charge.

As Joseph Pearce mentions in *The Crack in the Cosmic Egg: New Constructs of Mind and Reality*, "Our reality is influenced by our notions about reality, regardless of the nature of those notions." That means that to the extent we develop a point of view (a reality) that differs from our partner's point of view, danger increases that our core assumptions about many things will not align well with that partner. Down that path lives conflict.

Your current personality has been built upon wide-ranging assumptions about what is right and wrong, good and evil, safe and harmful, etc. However, as Gerard Nierenberg puts it in *How to Give and Receive Advice*, "Your reality is built on the sands of your assumptions."

Each of our assumptions evolved from a survival reaction to personal experiences. When you were very young, something happened that you didn't quite understand (because you were so young). You (as an infant) decided, *Well, I don't like what just happened, but if I do Y in the future, maybe X won't happen to me again*. Thousands upon thousands of tiny decisions like this one have formed the *you* that you are today.

Most of us are blind to why we act as we do. We are not aware of how we got to the way we are. This suggests that unless one or both of you are particularly insightful, neither quite understands why you do things as you do them and why many of your daily conflicts/discomforts arise in the first place. That's a problem.

It's a problem because one or the other (or both) of you is likely to react in ways that do not quite make sense to the other person. That is why so much of this book is devoted to helping you uncover assumptions, biases, or expectations hidden within yourself.

Much of this book explores communication concepts and offers ways to change how you speak with and listen to others. Along the way, we offer suggestions to avoid communication failures. In our experience, many challenging relationship situations get named *problems* because you can't quite figure out what went wrong. You can't quite identify it as one thing or another, it's just one more item in a long list of unresolvable issues. If you *could* discover the ways your many-layered filters have distorted the discussion topic, you might see the situation more as a challenge than as a problem. In that light, you would have a much better chance of resolving the issue.

We have interspersed some aphorisms (proverbs) throughout this book. They have a way of summarizing wisdom. For example, take the saying, "If you don't have what you want, you are not 100% committed to it." We encourage you to be 100% committed to no longer being an obstacle in your own path to better communication.

And that is a good place to leave this section.

Relationship issues

Let's discuss "the elephant in the room." We usually hear this term to describe sensitive topics that can't be broached. It is as though a baby elephant has moved into your relationship and it is being fed by your choice to act as though it doesn't exist. It grows each time you avoid discussing an emotionally charged topic. It thrives as each landmine is added to the list of things that can never be brought up. The elephant looms over you when one of the prohibited topics surfaces for even a moment.

Pretty soon, there are more topics you *can't* discuss with your partner than topics you *can*. The elephant has crowded you out. Emotional withdrawal accompanies communication breakdowns, as one or both partners act to protect their hearts from emotional pain.

This loop is not surprising. However, it *is* surprising that so few couples seem to recognize it for what it is: a loop of communication failure. Unless interrupted, this pattern can begin a downward spiral. In our experience, it is often the relationship's leader who declines outside help or introspective analysis. They usually claim to be perfectly happy, and any problem is being caused (or made up) by the other person or some external circumstance.

> Fresh communication skills can help to clean out the cobwebs of misunderstanding and misinterpretation that have grown to impact your interactions with yourself as well as with others.

Structures

We assert that Western culture contributes to communication failure loops. Traditionally, men have been the decision makers and women have been kept away from positions of power and responsibility. In a general way, common archetypes of boyfriend/girlfriend (or husband/wife) are laced with the seldom-voiced assumption that the man is the decider and the woman is the manager.

In addition, these archetypes are so prevalent and strong that few people consider other relationship options. And there are, in fact, many interesting options waiting to be discovered.

We absolutely know there is more than just this binary approach to relationships. The beautiful medley of possibility that arises from our LGBTQIA+ community challenges the preconceived and outmoded ideas of how we communicate. Traditional communication concepts have the burdensome filter of gender; this book aims to reduce as much of that background noise as possible. Just insert your own pronouns where you would like. Oh, and though our language often skews towards couples, please feel free to adjust in ways that acknowledge and honor any differences on your side.

Since we are bringing up alternative relationship structures, our personal favorite is the *executive leadership* model. We explain it as the CEO/COO structure. The CEO (of either gender) is outward-looking and guides the relationship. They are the visionary looking at a world of possibilities. Their job is to utilize their partner's strengths to accomplish more as a couple than they could as individuals. This concept is also referred to as the *one plus one equals eleven* model.

Looking a little more closely at the CEO/COO structure, the CEO (or leader) is tasked with making all final decisions. On the other hand, the COO (or follower) is responsible for keeping the relationship running smoothly and providing the CEO with the information and tools needed to make their vision a reality. This relationship structure works particularly well when someone who identifies as a leader is paired with someone who identifies as a manager. The manager keeps the household/business in order, enabling the leader to explore new paths/directions for the relationship.

Couples generally create relationship structures that suit their own preferences. While one is not inherently better or worse than any of the others, some are *much* better suited than others for specific couples. The takeaway here is that there are a number of established options to the traditional husband/wife relationship model.

Many modern relationships are called *egalitarian*. Egalitarian means everyone is equal and deserves equal rights. We believe that everyone is entitled to equality. We also believe that everyone has power. However, it is difficult to have equal *authority*. By authority, we mean the power or the right to make decisions. This includes decisions about what to have for dinner, which movie to watch, and even what clothing to wear. When there is a difference of opinion, it takes compromise to reach *any* decision.

We believe that relationships operate more smoothly when that authority has been clearly defined. If your partner is better at finances, then it is probably a smart idea to give them authority over finances. It is common in some cultures for the man to be in charge or head of the household. We do not believe gender is the determining factor for the *who is in charge?* question. We do find that defining who has a more authoritative role (the leader) and has a more supportive role (the follower) helps relationships run most smoothly. Succinctly, one person is given the authority to lead; the other accepts responsibility to follow.

Behaviors

When something surprising happens, you have a *reaction*. Reactions go by very quickly. Reacting to something does not threaten your relationship, it's just a recognition of surprise. Once you recover from the surprise (of some kind), you figure out how to deal with it.

Instead of dealing with the surprise by discussing it with your partner, you might decide to ignore it. Unchecked, this can lead to a pattern of *resistance*. You drag your feet; you don't clean the house or cook as before.

Resistance in a relationship is usually a cry for help. The resisting partner needs to talk. They may not *know* they need to talk, and they may resist their partner's efforts to draw them out. In most cases, this is because their partner is not a very good at speaking with them in tense situations.

Some surprise-triggered reactance is fairly common, particularly at the beginning of a relationship. Similarly, some degree of friction surfaces in even the best relationships. However, when relationships start to go south, resistance can turn into *revolt*.

Coordinating communication strategies between two or more upset people requires leadership. More than simple leadership, it requires leadership from someone who knows how to manage critical conversations. There are books on this topic that provide outstanding advice. Such books often fall within the general category of *Nonviolent Communication* (NVC). According to Marshall Rosenberg, NVC has two parts: *listening with empathy* and *expressing yourself honestly*. The NVC process succeeds when those involved focus on mutually beneficial outcomes.

At any rate, when tense situations arise, those involved will benefit when at least one person can take responsibility for leading a serious, thoughtful, truthful, and sometimes painful discussion. These discussions are necessary because each of us has somewhat different mental images (expectations) about what, exactly, our relationship is supposed to be—and even who we are supposed to be to our own partner.

Expectations come from the outside looking in. They come from movies, the Internet, books, TV, and from seeing other couples who appear to look so easily compatible and fulfilled.

Motivations

We want to touch on some common factors (motivations) that prompt people to live together and/or get married:

- Hot sex and passionate love

- Providing or receiving service

- Friendship and camaraderie

- Financial security and improved standard of living

- Procreation and child rearing

- Convenience or fear of being alone

- Social pressure or a socially accepted timeline

- You get the idea...

Obviously, the look and feel of your own relationship represents a blend of these basic motivations. As you live and gain life experiences together, the relative importance of these change a bit. In some cases, you grow closer and more stable with your partner; in other cases, not so much. In fact, relationship misunderstandings and miscommunication can often be blamed on mismatched relationship motivations. Translation: As time goes on, familiarity can breed contempt.

Here is an example of a motivation mismatch. Two people are going out on a date. One person sees this as an opportunity for romance, as they are romantically interested in the other. However, the other person views this only as a friendship date, as they are not interested in falling in love right now (or even with that person). If love is primarily motivating one person but friendship is primarily motivating the other, the evening's outcome probably won't meet expectations.

Successful relationships require the two (or more) of you to have similar motivations. Said another way: Do you and your partner(s) have a similar relationship purpose? Are both of you committed to maintaining that purpose?

By the way, since we're discussing motivations, you may find that your partner isn't particularly interested in practicing the techniques outlined in this book. You may wish to ask in advance *whether your partner wants an improved relationship with you*. If they do not, that suggests they're already on the exit path.

Risks

As Skip Chasey (a renowned presenter on relationship dynamics) often comments in his lectures, "If you're not *working* on your relationship, you really are not *in* the relationship." That applies to each of you.

We train and train for almost everything we do in life. We certainly train for our jobs/profession. Interestingly, there are some really important areas in life we seem *not* to train for. We don't train to learn sex techniques, we seldom take classes to be parents, and we have known very, very few people who have actually had classes/retreats about how to behave in personal relationships. As with most skills-based fields, the more training you have, the more competent you will feel when engaged in that activity.

How you handle the care and nurturing of your relationship largely depends on how the relationship is structured. The way the relationship is structured will affect (or control) the ways each of you deal with *upsets*. We're going to discuss upsets in some depth later in this book. Right now, we would like to discuss relationship structure.

You and your partner may want to determine who has authority over what, in order to ensure that you have common relationship motivations and a shared vision of the future. We recommend writing this down. We also recommend writing out an agreement about how the two of you will work through upsets and challenges with honor and integrity. Writing things down is important because people who feel unsafe in a personal relationship will be guarded and unforthcoming (we go into this in more depth in Chapter Three under "Beliefs").

You might also consider setting up a plan for sharing intimate feelings in a safe setting (see "Rules of Engagement" in Chapter Five).

To feel safe sharing information, we suggest establishing a practice where nothing said by either of you can be used against the other. Unless there has been an ethical breach, both of you should try not to react negatively to anything the other person says. This helps ensure emotional safety.

Relationships are tough, and good communication skills are certainly important. Here are a few subtleties to consider relevant:

- **Point of focus.** When shown a white piece of paper with a red dot on it and asked what they see, most people will say "A red dot on a piece of white paper." That's natural; humans tend to focus on the anomaly, on what is unusual about that piece of paper. Relationships have a similar risk. If one partner finds certain displeasing behaviors in the other partner, they may get distracted from looking at the good parts of the relationship and instead focus on parts that aren't working so well. *Red dot behavior* is the tendency to focus on the parts rather than the whole. Worse, the better the overall relationship is working, the greater the tendency to notice the few things that aren't. Obviously, it is a constant battle to overcome this characteristic of human nature.

- **Participant-observer bias.** It can be hard to see yourself. It can be a challenge to work on yourself because you can't tell if it's working—whatever the *it* is. Most feedback comes from others who see you change and comment on it. I (Bob) once heard someone make a profound observation. I don't remember who said it or when, and I have no way of knowing whether it's actually true, but it sounds valid. They observed, "You do all things the way you do one thing." While the superficial meaning is obvious, there is a disturbing implication. It suggests that if you don't like some of the ways you do things, you will have to work your way back to the core values/beliefs that affect the way you solve problems.

That is why trying to change yourself can be such a challenge: You've been perfecting your way of problem-solving for most of your life; deciding now to fine-tune the formula disrupts the status quo. Your inner mind won't like that and will feed you negative thoughts about your proposed project. You have to be strong enough to overcome your own mind shouting at you.

Various factors affect how much of your own behavior you can change. Most obviously, your own success depends both on the amount of time and effort you put in, and also how much you know about changing yourself. And, those changes will cause other changes that cause still more changes; it's a dynamic process.

Now for the bad news: The less self-improvement time available to you and your partner, the harder it is to make the changes necessary to alter your course. In this light, technology is your enemy. To the extent the two of you come home from work and turn on the television or sit at separate computers, you are missing opportunities to speak with, play with, and learn with your life mate.

- **Focus and intent.** You can alter your interactions with your partner by paying attention. When planning or executing something (just about anything), what you intend to accomplish and how focused you are on accomplishing it directly affect your success. Focus and intent alter the way you react to the world.

- **Self-talk.** There are techniques for replacing negative thoughts with positive thoughts and slowing or softening your inner voice. Your ability to be in the moment with your partner is improved when you are saying good things to yourself about yourself. We recommend Shad Helmstetter's book *What to Say When You Talk to Yourself*, as he includes some strategies that I (Bob) personally found very effective.

What you think you know

In the most real sense, what you know is only relevant if you can remember, access, and use that information. You may know a great deal but not know how to apply it. In that case, you are no better off than someone who doesn't know much.

There are two topics that relate to this concept: *visible and invisible knowledge* and *conscious and unconscious knowledge*.

Visible and invisible knowledge

This section tackles the cause of misunderstanding between people because one of them does not have the same background knowledge as the other. The listener *thinks* they got the message, but they didn't. One reason for this is that the speaker assumed the listener had certain background knowledge that they did not have. Thus, the speaker left out key information and was surprised that their partner didn't understand them. Another reason is that the listener *filled in* (or *colored*) the speaker's words with their own interpretation or perspective. The listener didn't quite understand the speaker, but thought they understood *enough* that they could fill in the gaps. Sometimes, this works; other times, not so much. In critical conversations, this little gap can lead to rifts, misinterpretations, and upsets.

Each of us has knowledge that is *invisible* to our partner. Some quick examples:

- **Business practices**. You may not have the same knowledge about business practices:

    - You may want your partner to use a business planning approach for a new project for the two of you. This doesn't

work out very well because the world of project performance, feedback loops, risk analysis, and system dynamics
are little known or unknown to them.

- You ask that your partner change the routing on an overnight delivery of three packages. The process fails because
you assumed your partner knew to specifically confirm the
rerouting information for each piece when multiple packages are involved.

- **Interpersonal skills**. You may not have the same knowledge
about working with people:

  - You notice that your partner is a little insensitive and/or
  rude when around other people. After a lot of probing, you
  realize that your partner prefers to work alone (vs. in a team
  setting) and has limited social skills.

  - You notice that your partner becomes reactive when stressed
  or challenged. After discussions, you realize they have little
  training in stress management or dealing with difficult conversations. You find they rely solely on personal experiences.

  As you'll see, *stress* (and strategies for reducing stress) come
  up repeatedly throughout this book. We mention it here
  as an important relationship issue that may be invisible to
  your partner.

- **Nature vs. nurture**. The best current thinking says that *who you
  are today* is comprised of about 40% inherited characteristics
  and about 60% what you have learned growing up:

  - *Nature* refers to what you have inherited from your parents
  that lives on as your default ways of doing things. You can
  think of this as your *prewiring*. It requires a great deal of
  work and conscious effort to move beyond that.

- *Nurture* relates to what you experienced and learned growing up. Your background probably differs from that of your chosen partner. Your motivations and beliefs grew from these experiences, and as a result, your adult actions in some areas seem foreign to your partner.

- **Gender differences and bias.** These topics have been so beaten to death that we will only briefly mention a few:

  - Men and women often grow up learning slightly different things. The trite way of saying this is that parents tend to teach boys "guy things" and girls "girl things." This includes telling boys they shouldn't cry and insisting that girls not get dirty. This way of passing down generational bias results in gender-linked differences in executive skills as well as heavily impacting our expectations of how we should communicate based on gender.

  - In our male-dominated culture, the fact that women have somewhat different knowledge bases and use slightly different problem-solving skills is made worse by the male tendency to discount what women say in many/most interactions. We frequently hear women comment that they make a work recommendation that is rejected out-of-hand by a male colleague, only for it to resurface some days/weeks later as the man's idea. In a heteronormative relationship, if the male partner is the leader, the female partner may feel she is not being *heard*, and that her needs are not being met.

Message: Education, work experiences, inherited characteristics, upbringing, and gender all conspire to give you and your partner slightly-to-extremely different views of the same topic/issue. Communication in a relationship becomes clearer as you identify and discuss these differences. Relationships are strengthened by learning to bridge differences in outlook and worldview. Furthermore, these skills lead to greater empathy towards (and appreciation of) other people's views.

As you expand your perspectives about people and life and increase your tolerance for other viewpoints, you enrich yourself and the world around you.

Conscious and unconscious knowledge

One of the greatest challenges when expanding your personal universe is that (as we just said), you don't know what you don't know. As an example, we could mention *depth-of-field calculations* or GO *stones*, and very few readers would know much about them. Nor do they need to. Under normal circumstances, most of us are perfectly happy not knowing much about things that don't interest us.

In a general way, there are four stages everyone goes through when developing competence in any field. Knowing about these four stages may help you assess the amount of training you or your partner will need when you encounter a new idea. Here they are:

1 **Unconscious incompetence.** You don't know something, but you don't know that you don't know it. Or, you think you know something, but you are wrong; you don't really know what you're talking about. (For example, only a small number of readers can explain why it is so hard to play a didgeridoo and fewer still care that they can't play one.)

2 **Conscious incompetence.** You don't understand some concept or skill. Or, you're trying to gain competence in some field. (Once you see/hear a didgeridoo solo, you may be motivated to learn how to play the thing.)

3   **Conscious competence.** You understand or know how to do something, but demonstrating the skill or knowledge requires concentration. The new skill or knowledge will probably have to be "chunked down" into manageable learning units that can take years to master. (You've bought a didgeridoo and finally figured out how to do circular breathing. Now, you've even started learning how to blend different tones/sounds.)

4   **Unconscious competence.** At this stage, you have had so much practice with a skill that it has become second nature. You can perform the task easily and without conscious thought. As a result, the skill can be performed while executing another task or two. You have reached understanding, and you're able to teach that knowledge or skill to others. (You're now teaching, performing, and making CDs with the didgeridoo.)

Look: Life in general involves a complex learning curve. You are not born wise. The more you learn, the more you realize that there is a lot more to learn. Here are the same concepts expressed elegantly as a proverb:

> He who knows not, and knows not that he knows not, is a fool; shun him. [Unconscious incompetence.]

> He who knows not, and knows that he knows not, is ignorant; teach him. [Conscious incompetence.]

> He who knows, and knows not that he knows, is asleep; wake him. [Unconscious competence.]

> He who knows, and knows that he knows, is a wise man; follow him. [Conscious competence.]

One of life's many tasks is to learn stuff. Life stuff, relationship stuff, work stuff. Unfortunately, the truth about a great deal of life's "stuff" is that you don't understand it completely. As a result, certain things you are very sure you know are actually different than what you know about them. Often, this happens when you are exposed to an idea or skill, and you think you know enough to figure it out without thorough research. For example, you might put together a set of Ikea shelves without the instructions and then find you've got vital parts left over. The item works, so far as you can tell, so you don't bother to take the time to figure out what went wrong—at least until it falls apart.

As a result, *the way to do x* may be objectively different than *the way you do x*.

> When areas you don't know much about include communication and leadership, what you don't know can, in fact, hurt you.

In this light, one of your life tasks is to increase your "correct knowledge" and reduce your "incorrect knowledge." In a general sense, correct knowledge is objectively verifiable (e.g. best practices, industry standard, benchmarked, etc.).

Our egos being what they are, we are often so sure we are right about something, it is difficult for us to *listen in neutral* (without prejudging) and consider that we don't know everything about the topic. Even then, the challenge of changing our existing habits to the (now revealed) better way to do something can be challenging, indeed.

Difficulties

Difficulties can come up often in life. They can be small or *huge*. Regardless of their size, it can be challenging to explain the kind of difficulty you're having.

This happens because the word *difficulty* means different things to different people in different situations. If someone says they are *having a difficult time* or *in a difficulty,* we can guess about their problems, but we do not really know what they mean unless they offer explanations. Furthermore, expressions such as *having difficulties* or *having problems* can be a personal code that means they are not happy with their emotional condition, but they prefer not to speak about it in detail. Without more information, you cannot know whether they are having a small hiccup or if something catastrophic is occurring. Message: Clearly define the weight others put on specific words in order to assess how best to understand what they need.

Difficulties have different causes and different solutions depending upon someone's nature. What you see as a rather straightforward task may be viewed as daunting by someone else. This section is meant to help demystify the concept of difficulty.

Difficulties of one kind or another can arise at any moment. Largely, they are up to how the individual views a task. Ten people can look at the same task and feel very differently about how *difficult* it is. Whether or not a task gets tagged as difficult depends on how the person views it. Usually it is triggered by one of the following categories:

- **Effort difficulty.** The task is simply hard. It can be emotionally hard or physically hard. You can't take a shortcut. (It can be difficult to make new friends or find a partner.)

- **Skill difficulty.** Some skills are simply hard to learn. It takes time. (In business, it's referred to as *time on task*.)

- **Luck difficulty.** Some results are attained through luck rather than conscious work. (Winning the lottery falls into this camp. To some extent, games such as poker contain both skill and luck difficulties.)

By the way, difficult assignments can be made easier by breaking them down into their component parts and putting parameters around each part. In the world of business, these are called *project management sheets, time-and-task sheets*, or *milestone analyses*. Once you write out all the steps and can see the actual scope of work, the task may appear less formidable.

You can build personal systems (often referred to as *protocols*) to manage projects. I (Bob) have used the same protocol for years concerning agreements. It works with adults and with children. In this protocol, an *agreement* is only reached once four distinct aspects have been defined:

1   **A statement of what is to be done.** "I would like you to make me a sandwich."

2   **A statement of how thoroughly it is to be done** (called the *conditions of satisfaction*). "I would like a sandwich for lunch. Please take one single piece of sourdough bread from the pantry and cut it in half. On one half, lightly spread some French's mustard. On the other half, please spread a light coat of mayonnaise. Add one slice of pepper jack cheese, one slice of deli roast turkey breast and one slice of beef pastrami. Place this on a paper plate and warm it in the microwave for one minute at 40% power. Once removed, insert about as much lettuce leaf as you have meat and cheese. Transfer the sandwich from the paper plate to a luncheon plate, add an ounce of Fritos and a half-slice of a Vlasic pickle."

3   **A statement about the time frame.** "It is to be served at 12:45 today."

4   **A statement of the acceptance criteria.** "Will you be able to prepare that sandwich and serve it at 12:45?"

Here are some additional guidelines that help such mini-contracts to succeed:

- Don't agree to a task unless you actually believe you can do it. Your word is your bond.

- If you suspect you can't complete the task the way it was requested, speak up before you agree to it.

- You must discuss changes in any aspect of the agreement *before* the agreement is accepted or as soon as the needed modification becomes apparent. You can't wait until ten minutes before the deadline and ask for an extension. Not fair.

- Work out in advance some consequence that is serious enough to be motivating, while also being appropriate for the importance of the assigned task.

Not too tough. The benefit of speaking the agreement is that it ensures that both parties understand and agree on everything that is important with the task. It removes doubt and fosters connection.

Larger (longer-term) difficult tasks involve different questions depending upon the type of difficulty you are encountering. For example, if you are taking on a challenge such as working on your personal relationship, you'll need to outline a plan of attack that is able to sustain you for years.

In such cases, we recommend you break down the overall project into short-term, mid-term, and long-term plans of attack. We suggest this for two reasons: first, completing each part of a lager project will make you feel successful; and second, you are less likely to procrastinate starting a modest-sized project than one you consider huge (and disheartening).

By the way, you can't treat all difficult tasks the same way. Some demanding tasks require acceptance while others require aggression; some require responsiveness while others require stoicism. Knowing the kind of difficulty (and how to approach it) improves your chances of successfully overcoming the challenge.

Here are a few words on various approaches/solutions to different difficult tasks:

- If the difficulty involves one-time luck, then you're either in luck or not in luck. Win/lose.

- If the difficulty is not a one-time affair, then you have to decide how much work it will take to accomplish the task without luck already on your side.

- If the difficulty is a repeated experience (such as communicating within a marriage), it helps if you do not rely solely on luck. This can mean improving communication skills, planning how you'll deal with upsets, and working to create an environment of supportive love. Translation: In a relationship, you have to make your own luck.

- If the difficulty concerns in-depth mastery of a skill (or a field of study), then buckle down and build your personal plan for success. Find people who are experts in this field, determine how they succeeded, and model yourself after them. Find a coach/mentor. The more study hours (effort) you put in, the more rewards you'll see.

- If the difficulty involves mastering a wide breadth of information to perform a task at a certain level of proficiency, be patient and focus on small gains. Celebrate little improvements. Embrace the tiny victories and build habits that enhance your efforts.

Luck

We want to stick a few paragraphs in here on the subject of *luck*, as your personal views on luck can affect both your worldview and your reactions to surprises. We consider luck to be *preparation meeting opportunity*. However, many people remove luck from most equations and instead believe that whatever will be will be.

Some luck happens only once. For example, you are running late for a time-sensitive appointment and the person you are meeting messages you they are running later than you are. Hurrah! Just don't count on it happening the next time you are late.

Some luck carries ongoing benefits. For example, your physical size enables you to excel in some activity or sport, or you're born with some innate gift and find yourself excelling in math, science, or music (to name a few).

Luck may have been involved early in the process of gaining excellence in a field, but it becomes less necessary over time. Imagine you've found yourself at the right place at the right time with the right training. Voila! You're in luck. Benefits and rewards follow you as you gain recognition for your expert knowledge and skills. Then, you hit a wall where greater expertise pays greater rewards. It is at this point that the requirement for luck has given way to the requirement for tenacity (another word for *effort*).

This is actually a nice way to close to this chapter, as Chapter Two presents some other perspectives and variables that affect your thinking and communication skills.

IT'S HARD...

It's hard to look inside yourself and see how you were built; it's hard to recognize what you have become. You have to really see yourself. To make change, you have to look at yourself and identify areas that need to change. Then you have to make those changes.

The more you understand how you work, the easier it will be for you to choose what to work on and what to ignore. This chapter explores personal variables that are well within your control and that have the potential to dramatically change the ways you relate to others.

We would like to start you out with some quotes from people who have captured aspects of this process in particularly concise phrases:

- "You will never find time for anything. If you want time you must make it." (Charles Robert Buxton)

- "Success is the culmination of failures, mistakes, false starts, confusion, and the determination to keep going anyway." (Nick Gleason)

- "Obstacles can't stop you. Problems can't stop you. Most of all, other people can't stop you. Only you can stop you." (Jeffrey Gitomer)

- "Success is the ability to go from failure to failure without losing your enthusiasm." (Winston Churchill)

- "Don't wish it were easier, wish you were better." (Jim Roh)

- "Today is always the most productive day of your week." (Mark Hunter)

Chapter 2

Perspectives and personality

NEWS FLASH! YOU ARE a very complicated person. So is your partner. So is your neighbor. So are we. Our backgrounds have made us who we are. Our current behaviors have been shaped by our unique interpretations of our experiences. That is, from infancy, something happened, it had an impact on us, we judged that impact to be good or bad, and we learned a mini-lesson that slightly modified our reaction to that person, place, or thing. Over time, our collection of reactions to our interpretation of events has created our current personalities.

This is one of our favorite chapters because we get to share some techniques that have helped improve our own communication skills. Veronica became certified in basic, advanced, and therapeutic hypnosis in 2003. She immediately began delving into *neuro-linguistic programming* (NLP). Bob became certified in basic NLP in 2009. Much of this chapter stems from our shared background in the world of NLP. We hope you find it useful.

We have divided this chapter into two sections: *perspectives on life* and *personality variables*.

Communication success is a product of who you are and how you have come to speak as you currently do. To change the way you speak, it might help to understand how you came to speak this way—to grasp the origins of the filters that pollute your capacity for clear communication may take some soul-searching.

Perspectives on life

We have compiled brief descriptions of some of the ways people differ as adults based on their own characteristics and upbringing. You will have to expand this list as you run across topics that are more relevant to your own relationships. We are just trying to get you thinking along these lines:

- Assumptions

- Upbringing

- The happiness set point

- Worth, value, and position

- Needs vs. wants

- Inclusive vs. exclusive

- Reactance and resistance

- Giving and receiving gifts

- The meaning of time

Assumptions

As quantum physics has observed, everything is made up of events and potential. Applying that to communication, what we know (and what we *think* we know) is comprised of our interpretation of events that have been happening to us thousands of times a day since we were infants. The knowledge we have assembled in this way governs our view of the world and also how we respond to the universe.

Remember: Your facts are built on the sands of your assumptions. And—we hasten to add—assumptions are only **your** personal opinions and perspectives. This is another version of *you don't know what you don't know*. However, this line of thought says that when you express an opinion based on what you *think* you know, your belief about that subject is expressed as an *unfounded assumption* or assertion that feels like absolute reality. Except it isn't; it's just your opinion about (or interpretation of) an event.

Note: If you want a fresh and surprisingly profound look at how cultural differences have long-term impact on individual behavior, we recommend Malcolm Gladwell's book, *Outliers: The Story of Success*.

Let's look at how people view relationships.

Some believe that fate determines whether relationships work out. They believe that relationships are natural-occurring pairings that either do or do not succeed. By adopting that mindset, they largely absolve themselves of personal responsibility for working on the relationship. After all, it's up to the gods!

In our experience, people who expect a relationship to be successful without work end up divorced several times for usually the same reasons. They are not looking at themselves as a part of the problem.

Others believe that relationships require constant attention and tending. This second group of people check in with their partner to be sure that person's needs and wants are being honored. They do this frequently. The fact that you are reading this book suggests that you are a part of (or want to be a part of) this second group.

In our experience, successful long-term relationships require a lot of effort by both parties. The more work you put into the relationship, the smoother it runs. When problems arise, it's often due to one person's assumptions regarding the meaning of what the other person said or did that turned out not to be exactly correct.

Upbringing

You and your partner's outlook on life will be similar to the extent you come from similar backgrounds. This includes such areas as social class, education, work experience, and travel. Misunderstanding and friction can arise in a relationship when there are large differences between the two of you. Background differences (like all unique qualities) do not make one or the other of you more worthy/valuable/right—just different.

At some point, you will find yourself in a situation where you care more about an outcome than your partner does. This happens all the time. One of you cares more about where to go on vacation, or the way to set the table, or how the closet is arranged, or how money is handled. If your partner does not care one way or the other, it's no big deal for them to go along with your preferences. However, there will be times when they care very much and don't want to do things your way. When you hit such a barrier, it's worth it to try to figure out *why* you care (and why your partner cares). On some issues, we suspect you will hear parental echoes ringing in your head.

Oh, and these echoes are not always benign. They have guided your behavior and strongly influenced your choices. This is part of why racism, sexism, classism, and such are still so deeply entrenched in our society. Propaganda, brainwashing, and indoctrination often start at home during our formative years. These concepts often become unshakable beliefs about how we feel the world truly is.

Our individual set of preconceived values, quick judgments, and often-biased assertions influence how we categorize other people upon first meeting. Our values cause us to decide how these "others" should be treated. At the most basic level, many of us make an almost immediate assessment of whether this new person is part of the "us" category or one of "them," an unknown and possibly dangerous or inferior, certainly separate group of human beings.

We make daily snap decisions about everyone we meet. Some of our judgments are values-driven prejudices that should not be there, but some are personal threat-assessments that are part of our basic survival instincts. Most of these snap judgments are based on our own hidden (and always biased) personal views of the world (in general) and of people (in particular).

If you're interested in uncovering those hidden biases, you and your partner can rate the following statements on a scale of 1–10 (where 10 means *I completely agree* and 1 means *I completely disagree*). By the way, chances are you will occasionally hear your parents' voices in your head as you read these:

- Sloppy body, sloppy mind.

- Television dumbs you down.

- Your word is your bond; it is the basis of your character.

- Dishonesty is a character flaw.

- All partners in a relationship should be transparent to the other; no secrets.

- The way you keep your house reflects the way you think and what you value.

- All people have worth.

- Some people are better than others.

- It's more important to be nice than to be smart.

- Most wealthy people either inherited their money or were simply lucky.

- Your way of dressing speaks to who you are.

- You can't go to bed angry at your partner.

- Raising your voice during a disagreement doesn't show anger, but passion.

- What you say to your partner when you're mad doesn't count.

- People who were born in the U.S. but speak with a strong local accent are usually uneducated.

- Your level of education is a sign of your worth.

- Men should be heads of households; women should follow.

- Women should get married and have children.

- Men need to make more money than their women.

- Women need to cook and clean.

Some people have picked partners with very similar views. For other couples, there may be anywhere from mild to extreme disagreement. Discussing how your partner feels about similar issues (and where they fit positively or negatively with your own thinking) can help you understand their life filters. We each have mostly-unconscious, complex, and convoluted judgment systems. Friction can fester within a relationship when there are ideological mismatches. You cannot predict when or how mismatches will express themselves, but they will. The next time you have an upset with your partner, consider exploring how some of your beliefs fed the upset.

The happiness set point

In order to understand why some relationships get into trouble early on, it helps to know about a topic that Veronica is particularly passionate about: *the happiness set point* (developed by Sonja Lyubomirsky). This theory is based on the scientific discovery that our genes determine about 50% of whether we are generally happy or generally unhappy. Set point theory states that another 10% is based on our circumstances (age, health, gender, education, wealth, etc.). The final 40% results from our voluntary activities and attitudes.

Here is how this relates to relationships.

When you first fall into lust with someone, you are full of excitement and expectations. Your happiness feelings are off the charts. You are having the time of your life. Your body is coursing with happiness and love hormones. It's good to get up in the morning, and you and your new mate probably stay up later at night than you should.

There is a grace period when people form a union. This is the time when *new relationship energy* (NRE) blinds you to little annoyances in favor of great sex. This can last months or years. However, at some point, your pre-relationship happiness set point returns. Your eyes are opened: You are likely to become more critical of your partner.

Hopefully, everyone in the relationship has been practicing open and clear communication all along. You have now reached the point where communication transparency is critical for long-term relationship stability. It is each person's responsibility to discuss areas that are producing a bit (or a lot) of friction. Each person must assess whether actions singled out by their partner represent core beliefs that are unlikely to change without effort, or only superficial opinions that can be easily altered with new/different information.

Worth, value, and position

Your underlying (and probably biased) views about your own *worth* and *value* interact with the ways you ascribe worth/value to others. If you have a great deal of self-confidence, you are likely to project a confident air of authority and control. However, your feelings of self-worth and value are somewhat situational. After all, a successful attorney would not express the same degree of self-confidence after being exposed for some kind of felonious act. Similarly, how you act is influenced by the setting you are in.

For example, if you are a schoolteacher, you are in the dominant position with your students, yet in the subordinate position with the school's administrators. Your behavior (the expression of your sense-of-self) changes as you interact with students or the principal.

How you *act* in the subordinate role in a specific situation depends largely on three things: first, how dominant or submissive your personality is; second, your attitudes about your own value and self-worth; and third, your views on how much the situation matters.

The takeaway is that your role in different settings can vary. Thus, the way you share information with your spouse is unrelated to the way you might disclose information to an investigating police officer. Most (but not all) people deal with authority figures quite differently than they do with peers. You can think of *authority figures* as those who actually have *fate control* over you. When you are involved with an authority figure, making a mistake or doing something wrong may have consequences you would rather avoid.

Those brought up to be very discreet and respectful around people with power, authority, or influence will speak more cautiously and reflectively than those who have been brought differently.

This little section is meant to expose you to concepts and ideas that may help you figure out how the next upset happened and what each of you may have to change in order to live together successfully.

Needs vs. wants

What is it that you really need? You probably can't get everything you *want*, so it may be worthwhile to identify what you believe you really *need*. Being able to rationally prioritize and graciously compromise are important components to communication generally and to a relationship's well-being specifically.

In the world of business, there is a prophetic saying:

> What you have is not what you want,
> What you want is not what you need, and
> What you need costs too much.

Obviously, there are costs involved in all relationships. There are emotional costs, intellectual costs, opportunity costs, and so on. In a relationship, if you combine the costs of your *wants* and *needs*, you may develop a cost overrun. Personal budget cost overruns usually lead to debt buildup on emotional or financial credit cards. Not good.

This budget-busting condition develops when you have a lot of *wants* when it comes to your partner but not a lot of discernment about what you actually *need* from them. Without that discernment, there is the risk of getting upset over something that you *want* but don't actually *need*. Here are some quotes that speak more to *wants* than to *needs* that we find insightful:

- "One half of knowing what you want is knowing what you must give up before you get it." (Sidney Howard)

- "If you don't get what you want, it is a sign either that you did not seriously want it, or that you tried to bargain over the price." (Rudyard Kipling)

- "If you don't have what you want, you are not committed to it 100%." (Unknown)

- "There are two things to aim at in life: first, to get what you want and, after that, to enjoy it. Only the wisest of people achieve the second." (Logan Pearsall Smith)

Separating *needs* from *wants* when it comes to your relationship influences how you react to one another. Once you and your partner discuss each of your needs, you have the opportunity to build a workable future. Your solutions may not live up to all of your fantasies, but they will be the best solutions with respect to a sustainable and satisfying relationship.

Inclusive vs. exclusive

Do you tend to like people, or do you tend to have judgments and considerations that limit those with whom you feel relaxed? Are you comfortable speaking with a panhandler? With a grocery clerk? With a physicist? With an elected politician? How about speaking with someone shabbily dressed and then someone who appears to have just come from a photo shoot for a fashion magazine? Do your friends tend to be quite different from one another or pretty much the same?

This issue of inclusion/exclusion affects your communication ability. Your ability to speak comfortably is linked to whether or not you wish to spend any time speaking with someone. *That* assessment is often driven by your prejudgments about whether or not you want to have anything to do with that person in the first place.

Karen Martin, an author and our friend, has a slightly different way of describing people who accept others and those who do not. She refers to *polka-dot* and *plaid* people. Polka-dot people see differences between themselves and others and will isolate or exclude many/ most people from being candidates for friendship by mentally placing them in circles that are isolated from their own. She observes that in many cases, polka-dot people socialize based upon those perceived differences and have judgments about a person's race, class, socioeconomic status, education, physical size/weight, group/subculture, manner of speaking, spiritual or religious beliefs, and so on. They may let snap judgments color their willingness to develop friendships outside their comfort zones. In a nutshell, polka-dot people are looking for differences and usually don't approve of them.

During a private discussion with Bob in 2006, she continued:

> Actually, I believe they decide they are inside the polka-dot with all of the other people who think and act as they do. It can be just as inclusive as it is exclusive. Polka-dot people are very loyal to others in the circle. In contrast to polka-dot people, plaid people find value or worth in everyone and appreciate people for their individuality and the different perspectives they bring to bear on life. They may actually accept an individual based on an interest or a view that is not congruent with any of their other values.

Veronica thinks of plaid people as a woven tapestry that intersects in beautiful ways and is strengthened by differences that are a part of the whole cloth.

> There are two kinds of people: those who want to get things done and those who want to be right.

By the way, some people use different phrasing to describe this polka-dot/plaid phenomenon. Veronica, for example, regards the world as being full of gaps and differences between us. People either decide the divides are reasons for separation or are opportunities to build bridges to connect them.

How secure you are in your relationships often relies upon whether you view the world (and ultimately, love itself) through the lens of *scarcity* or *abundance*.

The viewpoint of scarcity vs. abundance can be likened to your bathtub. For some, once that bathtub has been filled with water, it can never be refilled. Every time something good happens to someone, there is less water for everyone else. When something good happens to someone else, such people can become envious or jealous because there is now less for them. When something good happens to them, they become afraid. They feel there are fewer chances of something good happening for them in the future. For others, that bathtub is overflowing from a faucet that is always open. They believe there is plenty for everyone. The lives of those who consider life full of abundance create different relationships than do those with one eye on scarcity.

Additionally, some people view love as *conditional*, while others view it as *unconditional*. That is, those who put conditions on their love for another might think to themselves, *I will love you so long as you do/learn or grow/behave in these ways.* Those who practice unconditional love would say or think, *I love you, nothing you can do or say will ever alter my love for you; now—let's talk about what you just did.*

Some people see love as a scarce commodity. If their partner begins to make an emotional connection with another person, they feel as though they have lost the amount of love that their partner is now giving to this new person. Abandonment alarms go off in their head. Therein lies jealousy, stress, conflict, and even emotional trauma. In some cases, the partner who wishes to connect emotionally (not necessarily sexually, by the way) may develop anger toward their partner for such conditional love, the love that says, *I will love you so long as you only love me*. As you can imagine, such situations will cause some degree of emotional separation (for self-protection) and adds a layer of stress to their communication.

On the other hand, some people see love as infinitely abundant. Their partner is welcome to have multiple emotionally close friends of either gender. These people adopt an attitude that encourages their partner to have multiple close emotional connections because they believe it helps to keep their primary relationship fresh and focused. These people know why they are a couple and bring new ideas and experiences back to one another, further stabilizing their union.

Polyamorous relationships view love as abundant. For those not familiar with the term *polyamory*, let us explain. Some people believe that you can love more than one person at a time. They sometimes establish intimate, consensual relationships with two or more people. Such arrangements are called *polyamorous relationships*. This is not the same as cheating on a partner. Ethical polyamory is based on informed consent.

Reactance and resistance

Sooner or later, you are going to encounter reactance and/or resistance when speaking with someone. The difference between these words is important.

Reactance is your subconscious signaling a sore spot. You say something the other person didn't expect, and they react. Their eyes widen; their body stiffens. Without building up to it, you might trigger their reaction to say *no* to an idea. With knowledge and practice, you can learn to speak in ways that don't trigger reactance in others, as well as ways of calming a person's reactance. (See, for example, *Crucial Conversations: Tools for Talking When Stakes Are High* by Kerry Patterson, et al.)

Reactance is usually a temporary flare related to some hurt that may (or may not) be related to the current issue. You say something and the listener:

- Gives you a quick look of defiance

- Expresses surprise, exasperation, or disgust

- Rolls their eyes

- Immediately denies what you're saying

- Has a reaction stronger than warranted by the interaction

- Directly challenges and/or questions what you just said

This is particularly common when a new couple is still working out their power structure. They are still determining the areas in which one person leads and the other follows. Each person's authority and responsibility is still in flux. Repeated, exceedingly strong responses to minor issues can signal an underlying, unresolved issue that might be above your pay grade to address. Translation: It might be time to see a mental health professional.

Unaddressed reactance can transition to *resistance*.

Resistance can be unconscious. It can build up over time as a result of prior conversations/experiences with someone (or with some past experience). This is troubling. It is likely a signal that something fundamental is amiss. This requires some careful probing and questioning. Whether in a work or personal setting, it has been our experience that resistance signals one person's failure to hear/see/feel the other person's signals for help/relief in some area. It is easy to perceive resistance as a rejection. That's not always so. At least in the beginning, you may be able to do a better job of empathizing and objectively investigating if you don't take resistance personally.

Let's apply this observation to the world of personal finances. Your partner has no savings and shows little financial responsibility. You want to build a secure future. You have a strong financial background and offer to review their budget. They react poorly. In fact, they absolutely refuse. Rather than casting this as rejection, consider this an opportunity to explore underlying reasons for their strong reaction to something you meant as a loving gesture. There are many reasons your partner may be uncomfortable with the idea of sharing such personal information. It may not be about you.

Again, our continual theme: Communication is improved when you have good listening skills and can appreciate the world through your partner's eyes.

Giving and receiving gifts

This may seem an odd item to place in a chapter dealing with assumptions, but we have found it to be very important. Gifts are a form of communication. They are a form of acknowledgment, a way of saying, *I really like you and I'm thinking about you.* It is a tangible symbol of an emotional connection.

For many people, gifts are an *I love you* statement (for more on this, see "Love Languages" in Chapter Six). These people derive joy and pleasure from shopping for the gift, wrapping it, and finding that special card to include with it. Similarly, if they don't receive what they consider to be appropriate gifts for special occasions (or as special rewards), they may feel devalued. Their feelings are hurt.

Trouble can arise in a relationship in which only one person uses gifts as a love message. If the non-gift-oriented person misses the love message, they may not react as the gift-giver had intended. This is no small misfire.

When a non-gift-oriented person is surprised by a gift, it may trigger a number of negative thoughts:

- *I didn't get a gift for them.*

- *My gift isn't as well-thought-out as the gift I'm receiving.*

- *Where in the world am I going to put **that**?*

- *Oh, geez—we said we weren't going to exchange gifts, and I didn't get them anything.*

- *Money, money, ah, the expense!*

People who do not communicate love by giving gifts may view them as another piece of junk they have to discard or give away. These people often look at gift giving as an unwelcome social obligation brought on by a holiday or occasion, rather than an *I like/love* you statement. By the way, those who interpret gifts as messages of love do not necessarily require the gift to be expensive. A little *I love you* chocolate on the pillow at night can be a huge emotional boost for such people.

There is more to giving and receiving a gift than the act itself. In relationships, it helps to know the other person's language of love.

The meaning of time

Time is to humans as water is to fish—you don't think about it, but your life's journey depends upon it.

Interestingly, modern quantum physics has revealed that time is a human construct that does not objectively exist. In his book *The Order of Time*, Carlo Rovelli explains that time is a fairly modern concept. Humans first learned to accurately measure time so sailing ships could figure out where they were in the world. Interestingly, timekeeping was only standardized in the 1800s when trains began to make scheduled stops. Prior to that, noon was vaguely defined as *when the sun is overhead*.

However interesting its background, *time* plays a very real role in relationships. After all, if you tell someone you're going to call them at 3 PM and you call at 2:50 or 3:10, you have not called at the agreed-upon time. Interpersonal rapport—how well two people get along—depends upon each person's assessment of the other person's honesty and integrity.

Calling on time or being on time in general are examples of ways people assess whether or not you keep your word. Your relationship with time affects your relationships with others and thus enters the world of communication issues. As in: *I feel disrespected when you are late.*

Joel Bennett, author of the extremely meaty and profound book *Time and Intimacy: A New Science of Personal Relationships*, lists eight basic functions of time that can support or tear down a relationship. As these eight points are communication issues, we have listed them here in a shortened and edited version. When reading these points, please keep in mind that this book is about communication in a broad sense. You may be communicating with a friend, a co-worker, or your domestic partner. Regardless of the person and the degree to which you know them, this is a list of time-related issues that can affect clear communication:

1   **Disruption.** When you are involved in a meaningful conversation with another person and someone (or some event) interrupts you, the connection between the two of you is broken. Disruptions affect the quality of your bonding. This is true whether you are a child speaking with a parent, an employee speaking with a colleague, or an octogenarian reminiscing with your spouse. High-quality communication (as opposed to small talk) requires uninterrupted focus.

    For a conversation to be disrupted the way we are describing, those involved must be *engaged* and *present* in the first place. If one person is multitasking while speaking with someone else, they have already signaled a fundamental lack of interest in (or commitment to) the conversation. In such cases, one more disruption hardly counts.

2   **Scheduling.** We all lead busy lives filled with places to go and people to see. Where we go and what we see shapes our lives. All this running about depends on scheduling. You make individual and joint decisions to commit time to specific tasks and activities whether at work or at play. When you think about scheduling this way, you are really *time shaping*. If you have a significant other, the two of you work together to determine what you are going to do within a certain time frame, whether an evening or a lifetime. Working together in this way is good for relationship bonding. When you plan your future together, your relationship moves in that direction.

3   **Timing.** Because change is a constant, some times are better than others to have a meaningful conversation. While most adults

are sensitive about when to (and not to) say certain things in a conversation, it can be difficult to assess how your topic (or wording) will be received in relation to the amount of stress you and your listener are under.

We touch on stress at the end of Chapter Three, but the message right now is that the timing of when you say things improves or weakens your effectiveness as a communicator. Often in emotionally charged situations, the best communication path is to think and not speak.

4   **Rhythmic synchronicity.** We all have various rhythms—biological, hormonal, and sleep–wake cycles—and it helps to understand if yours are in or out of sync with your partner's. This affects your general success with communication, as synchronicity influences many aspects of life. It certainly affected Bob's relations with one previous partner, as he is a night person and she is a morning person. He found that it was more effective to bring up certain topics at specific times of day. Try to avoid bringing up topics that may be contentious or cause your morning-person partner to be worried about something just as they are going to bed.

5   **Pacing.** Pacing concerns the degree to which someone pays attention to voice tonality and pitch when communicating. Slowing your voice and dropping to a lower tonal register signals that this topic is important to you and you are being serious or reflective. Pacing also refers to the way you do certain things (such as prepare for dinner or actually eat your meal) as a form of communication. Slow pacing communicates care and attention. Fast pacing can suggest unimportance or distraction.

6   **Routines.** People get in the habit of doing certain things. Done often enough, outsiders looking in might think those repetitive behaviors mean you are in a rut. Some people design routines

and some people just fall into them. Chances are, the way you think, speak, and react are all well-established patterns. This matters in the world of communication. When you speak to someone, they are using their own routine listening habits to understand you as best they can, and you are using your routine speaking habits to try to get your message across. Sometimes this works and sometimes it doesn't.

All we can do is point out that the way you speak and the way you listen are so ingrained, they are invisible to you. You think you are a clear speaker and listener... but that is totally subjective.

7 **Transition.** As your relationship with your domestic partner (or with your work colleagues) matures, your own role will change in unexpected (and unknowable) ways. For example, cooperation levels may fluctuate, your interest in your partner/job may rise and fall, or your personal interests may change. The components that make us *who we are* are dynamic. Some people can spontaneously go with the flow better than others. You may have to modify your communication strategies based not only on your assessment of the other person's ability to tolerate change, but also on changes in your own communication skills.

8 **Time transcendence.** When things are going well for us, our heart is light and time passes quickly. When things are not going so well, our hearts are heavy and time seems to drag on forever. We all have had these experiences. Knowing this enables you to plan activities with your partner that promote lightness and love.

Time is actually a concept worth researching and discussing in some depth. Until I (Bob) read Bennett's book, I had no idea of the many ways time affects communication in general—and specifically affects the inner workings of relationships. I strongly recommend reading his book.

Even if you don't, the knowledge from these eight points (and other material in this book) can help you introduce *thoughtfulness* to your actions in order to create an environment where *happiness* thrives.

Personality variables

Many things contribute to who we are. Some of people know more about themselves than others; some actively search out little windows through which to view themselves. Over the years, we have collected a number of ways of thinking about others and ourselves. We are only briefly listing some here.

Note: To explore the following material in greater depth, you might consider the book *Unlimited Power: The New Science of Personal Achievement* by Anthony Robbins.

By the way, these thinking loops are called *meta-programs* in NLP. Meta-programs are seldom important in isolation; together, they paint a particular picture of you and the person with whom you are speaking. These can be discovered through probing conversation, which is why they are in this book. They include:

- Toward vs. away from

- Internal vs. external

- Sorting-by-self vs. sorting-by-others

- Process vs. product

- Matcher vs. mismatcher

- Possibility vs. necessity

- Independent vs. cooperative

Toward vs. away from

Some people choose a path because they are moving *toward* a goal. They are attracted to something. Such people become involved with someone for a range of positive reasons. In a general sense, they are likely to believe that they can have more in life with this person than without. This is commonly referred to as a *synergistic relationship.*

Away from people pick partners for quite different reasons. They want to avoid something. For example, they may pick a partner to avoid financial stress, or to avoid the social stigma of being single, or to satisfy parental expectations. This is how people enter relationships they really know are not great.

Here are other examples that may help you better understand your partner (or co-workers) within this mode of thinking:

- Some people make financial investments because they are motivated to move toward financial gain. Others avoid making financial investments because they are motivated to move away from the risk of losing money.

- Some people take jobs that draw them towards risk and become first responders, salesmen, or entrepreneurs. Others take jobs to keep themselves (or others) away from risk and become accountants, contract attorneys, or general practitioners.

- Some people date to move toward getting to know someone. Others date to move away from being alone.

- Some people exercise to move toward healthy living. Others work out to move away from weight gain.

As you have conversations at work and at home, consider whether you and your listener are aligned in the ways you approach (or avoid) life and life experiences. The closer the two of you operate in this dynamic, the more you can support one another. Bob is a *toward* person, but he lived closely with an *away from* person for many years. It was a challenge working with her, as most things other than staying at home involved some *risk*—risk of not liking the party, city, restaurant, or movie; risk of having to speak with someone. To her, risk meant threat and threat meant don't do it. They stayed home a lot.

My (Veronica's) relationship with Bob is quite different. We are both *toward* people. We view every misstep as an opportunity for better understanding and growth of our relationship and each other. Our lives are full of adventure and possibility. When things don't go as planned, we look for the lessons we can take with us to enrich our lives. Every moment is a fresh and delightful gift—that's why it's called the *present*.

| We are not risk-averse; we are opportunity-driven.

Different motivational approaches play out in conversations. If you listen closely, you may find that preferences and decisions are based on the toward vs. away from dynamic. One particular set of words stand out as revealing someone's preference. Some people are excited to **get** *to work* while others **have** *to work*. Whether you view tasks as *opportunities* or *annoyances* will color many aspects of how easily and happily you flow through life. Wording choice offers a significant clue to help you develop conversation profiles for the people around you.

Internal vs. external

This is a brief discussion about how people are motivated. The concept of personal motivation is often divided between those who are *internally motivated* vs. those who are *externally motivated*.

Those who are *internally motivated* look at what they accomplish and are either satisfied or dissatisfied with the result. They do not need anyone else to approve of their accomplishment or to acknowledge them for having done it. They work well in isolation.

By comparison, those who are *externally motivated* often do not feel accomplishment or success until someone has recognized their work (won an award, met a quota) or acknowledged them.

Note: While motivations may differ, goals may be the same. Some people think that one is better than the other, but that is the same fallacy as thinking that being a boss is better than another position. While neither is true, there is a catch: When it comes to thinking of yourself as internally or externally motivated, your self-assessment suffers from what is called *participant-observer bias*. That is, someone else may have to help you to understand your own frame of reference as you are likely too close to yourself to be unbiased.

Just to confuse the issue, the degree to which you are internally or externally motivated is situational. The most internally motivated person in the world can easily become externally motivated in certain environments. Think about being in the military and having to follow orders. Your success in advancing in rank depends upon what others think of you. Your own assessment of your performance is secondary. So these terms are amorphous. For our purposes, we are looking at this topic only as it relates to your communication skills.

These concepts concern how people react to completing a job or task—as well as how they initiate the next job or task. For example, while an externally motivated person may only work at their job for the paycheck, an internally motivated person might do the same job for free because it gives them satisfaction or fulfillment.

At one extreme, you can imagine internally motivated people persisting at a task they like even though others tell them they aren't very good at it. They don't care what others think. Something about doing the task fulfills them without needing external validation. At the other extreme, you can imagine externally motivated people working very hard at something they don't much like in order to win a trophy, receive praise, make more money, buy a bigger boat, etc.

Using opposing frames of reference without realizing it (and talking about it) may make it hard to understand your partner's actions and reactions. Taking the time to figure out how the other person needs reinforcement and applying that to your daily lives will increase their feelings of validation and value in your relationship.

Sorting-by-self vs. sorting-by-others

The concept of *sorting-by-self* or *sorting-by-others* is extremely important in communication theory. It often sits at the core of misunderstandings, hurt feelings, and upsets. In situations where someone is called on to make a decision that could affect others, those who think of themselves first give answers that reflect that thinking pattern and vice versa. Those who sort by others first consider the impact their statement would have on those others.

Here is an example of how this can play out at home:

- Person A sorts primarily by self. While out running some errands, they remember they need something that would take additional time not previously discussed with their domestic partner, Person B. They insert this errand among the others. They are so focused on running the errand that it does not occur to them to call home to let their significant other know of the changed plans.

Result: The errand-running partner gets home later than they said they would.

- Person B also sorts by self. They may be upset because they had expected their mate home an hour earlier. If this situation has happened before, this partner may become angry at not having been called/notified of the changed arrival time. In extreme cases (of which Bob has had ample personal experience), the at-home person may view this situation as a violation of trust: Their errand-running partner didn't keep their word about when they'd be home.

- Person B is angry because they feel they were not considered; Person A is remorseful that actions they perceived as trivial have caused this much anger. They were simply late—what's the big deal? Person B is questioning the other's integrity; Person A is questioning their partner's volatility and instability.

This is seriously not good. If allowed to fester, this type of continued misunderstanding can threaten the relationship.

Instead, Person A could learn to keep Person B informed about changes in errands and arrival time. Person B could learn to defuse those situations by asking emotionally neutral questions dealing with *intent* before choosing to become reactive and emotional. Rarely does a partner choose to do something they know in advance will be taken badly by their partner.

Once Person B understands *why* Person A was so late, the pair can work together to develop strategies to avoid similar future conflicts.

That being said, when both partners sort by others, making a decision becomes rather difficult. It can lead to the well-known loop of:

- "What do you want for dinner tonight?"

- "I don't care, what do you want?"

- "I don't care, whatever you want."

Understanding and communication will help these personality types have successful relationships.

Process vs. product

Conflicts over *how* a job gets done can sometimes be confused with the *sorting-by-self vs. sorting-by-others* paradigm we just covered. In the prior case, it does not occur to the sorts-by-self person that anyone else really cares *what* they do, while the sorts-by-others person cares a great deal about how others would interpret their actions.

When it comes to completing a task, some people care primarily *how* the job gets done, others care primarily *that* the job gets done.

For example, a manager who values process over product in a work setting might say: "You are to be at work for eight hours starting at 8 AM." They may care that your body is there more than they care about your output. At the other end of the spectrum, a manager who values product over process might say: "You are to get your job done by X date. I don't care whether you are physically in the office as long as you are completing tasks on schedule."

In a home setting, one or the other of you may want certain tasks completed in a particular way. That person would be considered *process-driven*. For example, a process-driven person may want towels washed and folded according to specific steps. If their partner is *product-driven*, they may not be very interested in following those preferences, as they don't see any improvement in the final result.

They just want to make sure that, at the end, there are clean, folded towels in the linen closet. The process-driven person may begin to feel dissatisfied with the results while the product-driven person is patting themselves on the back for completing the task. This is a simple example of how conflict may begin between process-driven and product-driven people.

This process/product dichotomy can lead to conflict. The product-oriented person just wants to get the job done. The process-oriented person wants that same job done in a certain way. They are irritated when that particular way is not followed. This situation arises when the person being asked to do something is thinking, *Okay, I agree this needs to get done, but it doesn't matter how it's done, so I'm going to do it my way.*

Here is another example with Person A and Person B:

- Person A asks Person B to do X project in Y fashion.

- Person B uses the Y approach only once or twice before deciding it is nutty (or unimportant or unnecessarily difficult).

- Person B changes the way they are doing X project from the Y approach to their own Z approach.

- After some time, Person A realizes that Person B is not doing X in Y fashion, and comments about it.

- Person B becomes bristly. They don't see any reason why X should be done in Y fashion, especially since they've now successfully completed the task using their preferred Z approach and achieved the same result.

Mismatches concerning how tasks are done—regardless of how they ultimately turn out—create stress. If conflicts are frequent, one or the other person may conclude that compromise is unattainable, sacrifice by one or the other parties is inevitable, or the two of them together are not good long-term relationship candidates.

If neither party cares how projects are completed (or they have elected to give up control so long as they *are* completed), then there is no relationship threat at all.

Bottom line: People are different; their reactions are different. In work and in personal relationships, people choose the degree of control they wish to exercise. The degree of control they *wish* to exercise and the degree of control they actually *can* exercise are often not the same. Relationship friction builds up when one person inhibits the other person's expression of control. This is another significant area that can improve or degrade a relationship.

Matcher vs. mismatcher

Are you hunting for common ground when you start speaking with someone new? Are you listening for things the person says that resonate with you? Are you trying to establish rapport? When you're thinking about your partner, are you thinking of the many ways you're similar? If yes, you are what's called a *matcher* when it concerns initial reactions to someone else. (We briefly visited this concept in "Inclusion vs. Exclusion". This takes the concept of *polka-dot vs. plaid* people a bit further.)

The opposite, of course, is a *mismatcher*. This describes someone who immediately starts cataloging ways another person is different from them. Differences such as regional dialect, word choice, dress, posture, clarity, vocabulary come to mind. Mismatchers typically ask themselves if they have enough in common to establish any rapport with this person. They are likely to ask themselves, *Why bother?*

That being said, some people use two or more refining methods for sorting others. They may use one form for initial sorting, then another form to note exceptions. That is, some matchers look for common elements in a person or situation, but also note exceptions. This is called a *matcher with additions for differences*. On the other side is a *mismatcher with exceptions to sameness*.

The latter looks like this: A mismatcher meets someone for the first time. Differences between them and the other person pop up in the mismatcher's head. But, as the two of them speak, the mismatcher starts to find common ground. They seem to like similar activities. They enjoyed attending the same conference. They both also appreciate x, y, or z. Maybe the other person isn't so bad; perhaps the conversation can be maintained after all.

A matcher with additions for differences will likely thrive in positions involving social interaction. They will initially identify with everyone they meet and seem relaxed and friendly. As their conversation moves on, this person may notice a few things that are not like themself, but they are not big deals.

A mismatcher with exceptions for sameness will be less comfortable in social settings. If they belong to social groups, those will likely align with some of their particular interests. By joining a group that appeals to their preference for sameness, they can overcome their initial tendency to look for mismatches.

The matcher/mismatcher concept is usually expressed as a *glass-half-full* vs. a *glass-half-empty* viewpoint. Friction can arise when you are partnered with someone who has polar opposite ways of viewing events and people—unless, of course, you've discussed your differing sorting styles with each other. By doing this, each of you can learn to use your strengths to support the other within the relationship.

Possibility vs. necessity

Okay, this is somewhat close to the *toward vs. away from* discussion a few pages back. However, this version has a slight twist. This is about enjoying the journey and not simply about the end result.

Some people start a task because they are looking for possibilities that might open. It is something they *want* to do, not something they feel they *have* to do. They are *pulled*, not *pushed*, into action. They are at the cause of their actions, not the effect of limiting doubts and judgments. These people search for options, choices, experiences, etc. Often, it's a gift when they do something for another, as they are doing it because they want to and not just because they have to.

On the opposing side, other people are motivated more by necessity. They do something because they feel they obliged to do it. They are not pulled to act because of a new possibility; they feel forced to take what the world has laid before them. When they need a new job, new house, or new partner, they take what comes around or what seems available. Fate controls their options and opportunities. Often, when they do something for another, it's a sacrifice. In a relationship, such a person may say they live in quiet desperation, feeling they have no control over their future.

Relationship stress can build up if one person operates from possibility and the other operates from necessity. As an example, if the person operating from possibility proposes a new project to the person operating from necessity, they (the possibility person) may be met with a reaction that falls somewhere between disinterested to uncooperative. The necessity person sees no *need* for the new skill. Obviously, this can be very frustrating for both parties. Frustration equals stress equals an unstable relationship.

Some people are pulled towards possibility as part of who they are; others are generally satisfied with whatever life sends their way.

Independent vs. cooperative

Because some people have such strong views about the rightness of their knowledge and ways of dealing with the world, they prefer to work by themselves. They may have trouble working in group settings. Others prefer to solve problems in a group and find it hard to work alone. Without leadership, they may not know what to do. Perhaps they get lost in the minutia, find it hard to make decisions, or have problems staying on task.

> Communication is not about *conquering*. Communication is about finding common understanding and achieving mutually satisfying results.

Similarly, some people like to take personal responsibility for the results of their work, while others prefer to share responsibility for any project or task. Blending these two, some people prefer to work with other people while maintaining sole responsibility for a task. They are in charge, but not alone.

It helps to know whether you are speaking with a *solo thinker* or a *group thinker* (or some blend of the two), because such knowledge can help you to understand the other person's work preferences.

When engaged with solo thinkers, your goal is to stay away from direct conflict and fold your ideas into the discussion. When dealing with group thinkers, your task is to be more decisive as you provide more direction.

In a general way, you have to give up the belief that *you are right* in order to hear what the other person is saying. We all tend to come into discussions believing that other people think as we do. When they don't, we assume they must be wrong.

This raises the question: Would you rather be right, or would you rather be happy? You can choose which battles to fight.

Many of us are surprised when we encounter people who do not think as we do. Many of us are also quick to offer help/suggestions. Since the other person also believes that their thinking is correct (and that it is *you* who has missed some step), this can lead to each person trying to convince the other that they are wrong. Neither person is listening to understand; both are listening for opportunities to change the other person's point of view.

In slow motion, a conflict of assumptions takes this form:

- Life is good, since almost every exchange you have with people is smooth. You believe this is proof that you are right-thinking.

- Suddenly, someone expresses a non-complementary view, which surprises you.

- You are surprised because your way of thinking has to be correct and, of course, your viewpoint is valid.

- You immediately begin helping this unfortunately misguided or uninformed person to come back into alignment with your right-thinking views. *After all*, you think to yourself, *a few quick facts should clear up their misconception about the topic.*

- When you sense resistance, you try harder to make them understand where their reasoning went wrong.

- You rarely (if ever) stop to check your own assumptions.

- The both of you get stuck in the same loop, thinking the other person is the problem.

This is *not* a recipe for winning friends and influencing people. We can summarize this flawed communication loop this way: People tend to listen to respond rather than listen to understand.

Unfortunately, this pattern (or sequence) excludes room for self-evaluation. We react based on our core beliefs. We don't look inward to examine our own fallibility. We simply push on, trying to help the other person realize their errors. But they don't feel helped. They feel judged and unheard.

Arguments tend to arise over differing interpretations of some event. You both feel that you are right, and actually, you both are. However, you are each right in the context of your personal backgrounds and experiences. That does not make you objectively correct. Once you understand that you are both entitled to different perspectives, the ideas in this book help to fill in the actions/behaviors to enable you to live peacefully with your partner—at least until the next upset.

Having different perspectives does not mean someone is wrong or needs to be "fixed." Your learning styles, personality variables, and life experiences simply give you different points of view.

FIVE CORE BELIEFS AND ASSUMPTIONS

These five selected points are only slightly modified from Franklin Veaux's online journal. We refer you to his discussion of "Relationship Principles" (see "Cited Works" in the *Supplementary Material*) for other pearls of wisdom and value.

1 Just because you feel bad does not necessarily mean someone did something wrong.

2 Just because you feel good does not necessarily mean that what you're thinking or doing is right.

3 Expectation on your part does not necessarily create an obligation on someone else's part.

4 Different people express love differently; learn to recognize the way others express and receive love.

5 Don't treat people the way you would like to be treated. Treat them the way they would like to be treated.

Chapter 3

Experiences and worldview

COMMUNICATION GLITCHES CAN ARISE from differences between the way you and others see the world. Everyone's worldview is based on their own upbringing and life experiences. The person with whom you're speaking (obviously) sees the world based on *their* upbringing and life experiences, not yours. Taken together, your past has created the way you are today; your past confines you to your current reality.

This chapter considers some areas that influence your reaction to things people say to you. We'll touch on the following four topics:

1   Love

2   Beliefs

3   Thinking

4   Upsets

When you discuss these topics with others, you may be surprised both by how similar and dissimilar their views are from yours. As previously mentioned, differences in background and upbringing produce adults with very distinctive opinions or views that affect communication success or failure. It's not that one of you is more right or wrong than the other—just different. You're simply not aligned. Being more aligned generally results in smoother communication. Translation: These are topics you may want to learn to understand more about yourself and your significant other.

Love

This brief section is intended to broaden your views about the concept of love in order to increase your awareness of communication subtleties when emotional issues arise about your relationship.

Aspects of love

In a very general way, love can be viewed as a triangle. Each person's paradigm of love has some blend of three elements. This particular mix of romance, friendship, and self-worth gives each relationship its own unique characteristics:

1   **Romantic love** (eros). Love based on passion and/or romance; may be sexual in nature.

2   **Affectionate love** (philia). Affectionate love and possibly friendship; generally less sexual.

3   **Self-love.** Self-esteem; self-knowledge; general sense of self-worth. Lack of self-love may cause issues such as self-sabotage, difficulty accepting love, codependence, etc.

Since many people consider *service* to be an expression of their love, we propose adding it as a form of *love by choice*. Service as an expression of love includes examples such as: volunteering for charity work; running for public office; or cleaning public parks and roadways. Unlike romantic love where people tend to get caught up in emotions, service represents a "purer" choice to love.

The triangle has now become a pyramid.

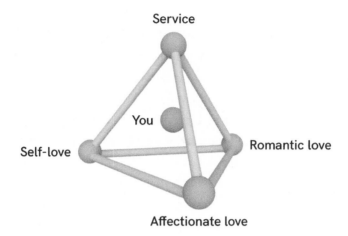

Everyone's location in the pyramid is different. Sometimes differences are unimportant; sometimes they are profoundly important.

Misunderstandings about the kind of love you have for one another can lead to hurt feelings. The point of this, though, is that as long as you are inside the pyramid, you are in the relationship. This is another area where couples can benefit from thinking about and discussing the kind of love they feel and offer towards one another (and the purpose of their relationship). It is also important to explore what each of you has to do so the other person recognizes and feels your love for them (see Chapter Six, "Love Languages").

TO LOVE VS. TO BE IN LOVE

Think of it this way: You love your children, but you are not *in* love with them; you love your parents, but you are not *in* love with them. It sometimes happens that you love someone, whereas they are *in love* with you (or vice versa). This subtle difference can cause the in-love partner to feel they are not getting back the same emotional commitment they are putting into the relationship. Unchecked, this can lead to upset and conflict.

In psychology, the *love vs. in love* scale is referred to as a *scale of emotional involvement*. Obviously, people in relationships have various levels of emotional attachment. For some, factors such as fulfilling an emotional or financial need outweigh the need for romantic connection. Whether romantic attachment is important in the relationship depends upon a person's motivations for being in the relationship.

Incentives

While most pairings result from sexual chemistry, not all relationships are sex-based. People have their own reasons for starting and remaining in relationships. We know a man who chose his partner because he wanted help changing some habits he knew she could change. We also know women who pick partners who dote on them and fill a daddy-type role. We also know gay men and lesbians who are married to each other to provide social cover in our heteronormative culture.

People may not understand what motivates them to pick certain partners. It's difficult to look at yourself and say, *I'm really looking for someone who can provide financial security more than someone who provides passionate, romantic love.* This is not an easy conversation to have with yourself. However, it is critical to know what is important to you and whether your partner can fulfill your needs.

For example, I (Veronica) require a stable and grounded partner. For years, I had a partner who placed a lot of importance on spontaneity and excitement. In the beginning, I found this thrilling. With time, his lack of stability made me feel unsafe and off balance. In turn, my partner felt stifled and judged. These types of fundamental mismatches do not work very well.

If a couple intends to stay together, they will need to know their own and each other's motivations. To make this discussion even more tricky, personal motivations may shift over time. This shift in motivations can reflect whether needs are (or are not) being met. They can also shift as people grow and change.

Ask yourself what motivates you to seek (or remain) in a relationship? What does this person offer you that enriches your life? What strengths do you bring into your relationship that enrich *their* life?

Conclusion: Motivations influence communication. Communication is what holds the relationship together.

Intentions

While some communication is casual and filled with small talk, other communications are influenced by the speakers' intentions. Here, the question is whether you even know each other's intentions.

First example: It's after work. You and your partner are at home. Customarily, your intention is to reconnect emotionally by sharing anecdotes about your workday. However, today you would rather not talk about your work shift, so you are not fully engaging in the conversation. Actually, you think you should start preparing your partner about some serious work-related issues, but you are afraid of their possible reaction. So, your intention has shifted. You are not quite listening to what your partner is saying. You are not being very direct, or you are not sharing your day. Your partner senses that something is different but can't figure out what's wrong. In self-defense, your partner's intentions have shifted from sharing to self-defense. They erect emotional barriers. As both partners have now withdrawn emotionally, the rest of the evening is a disaster.

Second example: Two people knew one another for about five years and even lived together off and on for another five years before getting married. Both had satisfying careers and quite a bit in common. He just loved being married to her. When the two of them turned 35, the wife suddenly declared she wanted children. This was a huge surprise, as the husband was not expecting to have children, had never discussed having children, and didn't like kids. He cautioned her that he'd go along with her wishes but would not guarantee a good outcome. The man had married the woman because he loved being with her. Once children were involved, the relationship focus shifted from each other to raising the children. They divorced some time later.

Intention is a key factor that affects the quality of your relationship.

Beliefs

Authority and leadership

Authority can be a tricky subject. In some settings, people are declared to have authority. For example, someone might start a business and be the president and CEO. Clearly, they have self-appointed authority. However, having authority is not the same as *knowing how to use that authority* competently, responsibly, and ethically. There is an important distinction between declared authority and earned authority.

This distinction most visibly affects couples when tough choices arise, and someone has to make a crucial decision.

Let's stay with the decision-making conflict for a moment. In most relationships, we find ourselves drifting into roles. In this case, imagine you have found that one person in the relationship isn't particularly comfortable making big decisions. Or perhaps one of you thrives on taking that responsibility. We don't care which camp you belong to—either way, we suggest discussing and resolving decision-making duties in your relationship. That way, each person knows their roles, responsibilities, and how and when to act.

Note: Authority within the relationship will probably shift depending on the topic. That is, one person may take the lead for financial planning and execution and may not take the lead in other areas such as childrearing, house maintenance, trip planning, etc.

Values

The process of clarifying your values opens a door to your motivations and behavior. Your parents and early education largely set your values. They affect the way you think, communicate, perceive the world, and treat others. If your parents were friendly and outgoing, chances are you are too. If they were introverted and guarded, there is a good chance you are as well (unless you've worked very hard to overcome that patterning).

People get satisfaction when they live in accordance with their values. Conversely, people may not notice when their lives are *not* aligned with their values, but they will have a constant sense of dissatisfaction. For example, if you are stuck all day in an office despite valuing fresh air and physical exercise, you are going to wish you could change jobs. You may not realize the underlying issue is lack of fresh air and exercise, but you know this job doesn't make you happy. Another example: If you value clear communication but find yourself interacting with people who hide their emotions and disguise their intentions, you're going to be uncomfortable.

In a few pages, we provide a list of value words. Values are your principles or standards of behavior; they are what is important in your life. You may want to spend a little time actually digging below the superficial meaning of these words to explain exactly what they mean to *you*. This is an important exercise, as values shape your beliefs and behaviors.

Definitions of most value words depend upon your belief system. Your belief system underpins your worldview. Unsurprisingly, other people may have quite different interpretations and reactions to the same value word. These differences are instructive—in subtle and also obvious ways—as most of us have different backgrounds.

ACCOUNTABILITY AND CHANGE

You might at first think it odd to include a discussion about accountability and change in a section on values, so let us explain. We all change throughout our lives. As our values develop and mature, the way we are in the world also changes. To point out the obvious, the person with whom you started a relationship (however many years ago) isn't the same person with whom you are now living. You both have changed in uncountable ways. But, this is where accountability and values come into play. As some people get older, they become more autonomous. They are less accountable to others. However, as other people get older, they become more dependent on others— more accountable for their actions and time.

So, here is a question: Are you sensitive to the fact that everyone (including yourself) has changed from how they were last month/ year? Some changes are profound. Others, not so much. We tend to see ourselves and others as though cast in amber.

You can see how accountability and change can be linked—but there are other major variables. For example, your own relationship with change has a strong influence on how roughly or smoothly you work through unexpected occurrences (such as getting fired or experiencing a natural disaster). Here are some questions that might help you better understand your feelings about change:

- Do you seek or resist change? Can you explain to yourself what positive or negative charge surrounds *change* for you? I (Bob) knew a man who not only changed jobs, he also changed fields about every five years. He used this as a way to continue learning and growing mentally.

- Do you go *toward* or *away from* necessary change? For example, do you go to the doctor when you suspect something is wrong or do you put off scheduling an appointment? We know many people who float upon the river of denial when it comes to medical issues. When they suspect something may be medically wrong with them, they specifically avoid seeing a doctor.

- How willing are you to change your small-scale behaviors? Getting more exercise is a good example. Will you park your car further away from stores? Are you willing to take the stairs instead of an elevator?

These are powerful questions, and the way you answer them reveals information both about your views of the world around you and also about the way you approach problem-solving.

VALUE WORDS

Take a look at the following values chart. Pick the five values most important to you. Ask your partner(s) to do the same. Prioritize them and share the results.

When you share common values, you are also more likely to have a stable relationship.

Abundance	Contentment	Fun
Acceptance	Cooperation	Generosity
Accountability	Control	Goodness
Achievement	Creativity	Gratitude
Adventure	Daring	Growth
Advocacy	Decisiveness	Happiness
Altruism	Dedication	Hard work
Ambition	Dependability	Health
Appreciation	Diversity	Honesty
Balance	Discipline	Honor
Beauty	Elegance	Humility
Boldness	Empathy	Humor
Calmness	Encouragement	Inclusiveness
Caring	Enjoyment	Independence
Challenge	Equality	Ingenuity
Charity	Excellence	Inner harmony
Collaboration	Fairness	Inquisitiveness
Commitment	Family	Insightfulness
Community	Fitness	Inspiration
Compassion	Flexibility	Intelligence
Competitiveness	Freedom	Introspection
Consistency	Friends	Intuition

Joy	Perfection	Sensitivity
Justice	Playfulness	Serenity
Kindness	Popularity	Service
Knowledge	Power	Spirituality
Leadership	Preparedness	Stability
Learning	Proactive	Strength
Legacy	Professionalism	Structure
Love	Punctuality	Success
Loyalty	Reason	Support
Mastery	Recognition	Teamwork
Mindfulness	Relaxation	Thankfulness
Morality	Reliability	Thoroughness
Motivation	Resilience	Thoughtfulness
Nature	Respect	Timeliness
Obedience	Resourceful	Tolerance
Open-mind	Responsibility	Traditionalism
Optimism	Restraint	Trustworthiness
Order	Risk-taking	Truth-seeking
Originality	Safety	Uniqueness
Passion	Security	Unity
Patriotism	Self-control	Variety
Peace	Self-reliance	Versatility

As you begin this exercise by reading the value words, you have to get past your initial reaction to think something like, *Equality—yes, I definitely believe in equality*. Take this challenge seriously. Ask yourself probing questions aimed at finding the heart of each value. Avoid yes/no answers. Explain, expand, and discuss. Be thoughtful.

This is actually a very challenging process. Not many people are willing to go through it on their own or with their partner. However, you will benefit from it. You will come to know yourself better.

Find your common values and develop goals to grow closer in those directions. We assert that, as you work in tandem, you will find a greater sense of unity and relationship satisfaction. For example, if you both share the value of *spirituality*, you might set up a private space for meditation. You then might explore and practice meditation techniques together. If you are thinking about a vacation, perhaps you would consider a spiritual retreat. As you help each other, you will be able to grow more as a team than you would separately.

This material affords you the opportunity to explore a world of little doorways into yourself and your partner. We believe you will better understand your own motivations after working through this list.

APPLYING VALUES

Your values affect how much you care about some topics—such as communication as an abstract concept. They also have an impact on how you feel about people, what you say to them, and how you react to what they say to you.

While the first step toward change involves identifying your key values, the second step involves translating those values to action. This is really material you have to do on your own, but here's a brief made-up example for someone who values *self-control* despite being prone to outbursts:

What do I want?	How will I do it?
I want to keep my emotions and impulses in check	I will learn and practice skills for dealing with my feelings, particularly those that sneak up on me
	If I have not made changes on my own within six months, I will seek professional help

Intentions that align with your values happen when you decide to express and magnify those values. Intentions are your action plan. People can become unfulfilled when their life plan is not aligned with their values. For example, if *knowledge* is one of your values, then you might set the intention of taking some online courses. Aligned intent starts with your values and become a statement about how you want to show up in the world. They are guideposts for who you want to be and how you want to show up, rather than what you want to do or accomplish.

If you are in a relationship, working through this list together may reveal a range of new possibilities to explore. Communication within your relationship will improve to the extent that you understand your own and your partner's values. You each have goals, and together, these goals should support the intent and purpose of your relationship. You strengthen your understanding of one another (and stabilize your relationship) when you work towards mutually derived goals. Working toward your goals gives you a rewarding reason to wake up in the morning—other than just making a paycheck.

By the way, there is risk involved with losing sight of your goals. If it is directionless, your relationship is likely to *drift*. It may drift from your initial intentions, goals, and dreams, and end up being swallowed by the routines of everyday life. As with most things in life, it is more difficult to retrieve something that has left you than it is to keep it from going away in the first place. It's easier to keep your relationship on track through communication and goal setting than it is to rebuild it after you have drifted apart emotionally.

Thinking

Misunderstandings

Our minds don't distinguish between what *really* happened and the way we have *reconstructed* the event as having happened. Thus, unless you are a skilled and impartial observer, your version of reality is pretty much a subjective fiction.

As psychologist Carl Jung observed, we *project* our life experiences onto our interpretation of what we perceive happened (see Chapter Four for specifics on projection). Often, this leads us to make what Pace and Kyeli Smith call *the usual error* by believing that other people think (or problem-solve) as we do.

Assumptions can contaminate discussions between people. A common pattern looks like this: Something happens → Each person assigns (different) meanings to the event → Biased individual realities get set by each party → They can't agree about what happened.

We have all seen people react in unexpected ways to something we have said or done. We don't know what set them off, but we certainly had not expected their response. We are left wondering what happened. Perhaps some unknown and unresolved personal issues triggered their reaction. Or maybe they misinterpreted the situation and are reacting to their own (very different) narrative. In our experience, people sometimes change the story of what happened so much that you can hardly recognize it's the same episode.

In fact, it's quite possible for your emotional baggage to take over a conversation. While we don't mean to sound melodramatic, you might think of this person as *not quite in their right mind*. Their thinking may seem a little irrational. In extreme cases, you may say *A*, *B*, and *C* while they are responding to *stone*, *35*, and *hay*.

It's at this point that you must be very, very careful not to further escalate the situation. It might be a good time to stop the current discussion and take a much-needed break. You don't want to start probing for the cause of the upset when the other person is already triggered. It is not the time to buy a one-way ticket into their land of imagination (beyond there be dragons and landmines).

Here is something I (Bob) actually experienced as an example of the kind of conversation you want to avoid in the heat of a really bad emotional meltdown:

- Person A says, "I've had enough; we're done!"

- Person B takes this to mean the relationship is over and says, "Fine!" They gather a few belongings and leave.

- Person A is in astonished shock. They didn't want their partner to go away; they only meant they were done arguing.

- Person B didn't really want to go, but they thought they were being told to get out.

- Both people are fuming and hurt. What a mess.

Heated miscommunication can lead to odd outcomes neither person wants. It's not that one or the other person was at fault, exactly. When two people connect, they create a new entity called *the relationship*. It has its own distinct energy pattern with unique challenges and opportunities. It can deteriorate before you even realize you were heading in such a direction. It also has its own set of communication rules based upon the participants. It can take a long time to figure out what they are.

Thinking styles

How you think and reach conclusions affects how you communicate and solve problems. Your thinking and working styles influence your communication preferences—and your communication preferences influence your working preferences. For example, if you are an introvert, your working style is likely to differ from someone who is an extrovert. Knowing your own thinking and working styles helps you to control yourself when working with others.

As we are not psychologists, we'll keep this section short and send you off to do more exploring on your own.

Taking a very broad view, *linear thinkers* (people who tend to go from *A* to *B* to *C* to *D*) are quite different from *branch thinkers* (people who go from *A* to *stone* to *zebra* to *D1*.) This can be either very good or very bad.

If the two of you start with the same *A* but one of you reaches a **better** *D* (e.g. *D1*), then branch thinking is working for both of you. If the two of you start at the same *A*, end up with *library* rather than *D* or *D1*, and *library* is a workable and mutually agreeable solution, then all is well. As long as the two (or more) of you are coming up with complementary solutions, everything is fine. The solution could be *D*, *DI*, or *library*. A problem arises when *DI* or *library* conflicts with the other person's desired outcome.

I (Bob) once lived with someone who often came up with a *related* conclusion, just not a conclusion he wanted or needed.

While we do not need to control our partner's thinking style, we *do* need to be able to discuss their conclusions. Sometimes we get caught up in trying to figure out *how* our partner thinks differently—and miss the spectacular conclusions they're offering us. Often, more than one possible path is revealed when there are two (or more) people involved in the decision-making process. It's great if we both get to *D* or *DI*. However, if one of us gets to *D* and the other get to *library*, maybe we need to do *D* in the library. You might say to your partner, "Let's speak about this different conclusion so I will have more information to help me make a decision."

Great books in these areas include:

- **Lateral Thinking: Creativity Step** by Step by Edward DeBono. (Note: DeBono has a number of books out on thinking, e.g. *Six Action Shoes*.)

- **Thinking Better: A Revolutionary New Program to Achieve Peak Mental Performance** by David Lewis and James Greene.

- **The Ideal Problem Solver: A Guide to Improving Thinking, Learning, and Creativity** by John D. Bransford and Barry S. Stein.

- **Teaching Thinking Skills: Theory and Practice** by Joan Boykoff Baron and Robert J. Sternberg.

The way you think also affects how well you get along with those who are listening to you. It's a matter of rapport. People tend to get along best with people who think like them. Large differences in thinking styles can doom a relationship. We know a number of such cases. If one member of a team just doesn't "get it," they may be singled out and discounted by other team members. A person's thinking style goes to the core of their being. How you think (and how you deal with those who don't think like you) is a major interpersonal issue.

In their book *The Art of Thinking*, Allen Harrison and Robert Bramson detail five distinct thinking styles in Western society. We are particularly fond of this book because their descriptions of these thinking styles—and ways of working with people who think in each of these patterns—are so pragmatic and helpful.

The authors found that most people prefer one or two of five *inquiry modes*:

1   The *synthesist* sees likeness in apparent opposites. They are interested in change.

2   The *idealist* seeks ideal solutions. They welcome a broad range of views.

3   The *pragmatist* seeks the shortest route to payoff. They are interested in whatever works.

4   The *analyst* is looking for the one best way. They are interested in data-heavy, scientific solutions.

5   The *realist* relies on facts and expert opinions. They are interested in concrete results.

These basic thinking styles are strongly influenced by the thinker's fundamental beliefs. These beliefs channel people to think about things in a specific way. To use contemporary examples, it's hard for most Americans to understand the logic and value sets of North Korean leaders. In exactly the same way, it's hard for North Korean leaders to understand the value sets and belief systems that make up life in the U.S.

Harrison and Bramson give everyday examples to produce a hands-on guide to teach you how to unbind your mind from narrow thinking. This is useful, yes? After all, who wants to be accused of thinking narrowly? Seriously, though, this is important material. Your ability to communicate clearly with someone depends, to a large extent, on whether you are able to interpret and understand *their* thinking style.

We recommend this book, as it is intended to help you select effective strategies for asking questions, making decisions, getting along with people, and solving problems. By learning *why* you think the way you do—and understanding the thinking styles of others—you will be better able to get past obstacles and turn conflict into cooperation.

Cognitive distortions

This material has been adapted from *Feeling Good: The New Mood Therapy* by David Burns. I (Bob) like this book; these ten bullet points helped me to understand *thinking problems* that come up every day. Forewarned is forearmed, and such.

1 **Overgeneralization.** The person presents things in black-and-white, all-or-nothing terms. This is the *throwing the baby out with the bathwater* mistake. For example, "Okay, you don't like the way I cook rice. Fine! I'll never cook rice for you again!"

2 **Mental filter.** The person picks out a single defect and dwells on it. Over time, their vision of reality becomes darkened, like the drop of ink that colors an entire beaker of water.

3   **Disqualifying the positive.** The person insists that some positive experience doesn't count for some reason or other. They dismiss something positive in order to maintain a negative belief that is contradicted by everyday experiences.

4   **Jumping to conclusions.** The person makes a negative interpretation of a situation without objective facts to support their conclusion. Here are three distinct types:

   1   **Mind reading.** The person arbitrarily concludes that someone doesn't like them simply because they didn't receive a smile when they walked into the room.

   2   **Projection.** The person projects personal beliefs, behaviors, fears, or insecurities onto another person, then reacts to them. For example, "I don't like people coming to my house, so I don't go to anyone else's house."

   Note: This is a common and pervasive issue that bears a lot of thought and attention. For more on Jungian projection, see Chapter Four.

   3   **Fortune telling.** The person anticipates that things will turn out badly, and then feels convinced that their (unrecognized) prediction is already an established fact—and reacts to it that way. For example, "Oh, you're a drummer in a band? I've heard about guys like you. I think I'll save myself some heartache and pass on this date."

5   **Magnification, catastrophizing, and minimization.** The person exaggerates the importance of things (such as a personal *oops* or someone else's achievement) or they inappropriately shrink things until they appear tiny (such as their own desirable qualities). For example, "My boyfriend has come home late all this week. I suspect either he's lost interest in me or is cheating on me."

6   **Emotional reasoning.** The person assumes that their negative emotions reflect the way things really are. This is the *I feel it, therefore it must be true* syndrome. For example, "I'll tell you: I've had a horrible week at work. Clearly, this isn't the job for me."

Note: In the language of *transactional analysis* (TA), this is the *child voice* speaking. See "Ego States" in Chapter Six for more.

7   *Should* **statements.** The person uses *shoulds* and *shouldn'ts* to create rules for themselves and others. *Musts* and *oughts* are in the same category: The only two possible options are to pass or to fail. Such self-talk reinforces their own pessimistic view of their life. For example, "My doctor says I'm prediabetic and that I really should lose weight" (as opposed to "My doctor says I prediabetic; this is just the motivation I need to lose weight").

When someone directs *should* statements towards others, it is usually because they feel anger and resentment towards someone who is breaking the rules. For example, "You should have called me before deciding that you were picking up Thai for dinner."

Note: In the language of TA, this is the *parent voice* speaking and is likely to trigger a defensive child voice reply, such as: "You *never* like what I bring home for dinner, why should I bother asking?!"

8   **Labeling and mislabeling.** The person attaches a negative label to themselves (or others) as they describe an event. Mislabeling often involves emotionally loading their judgment. For example, "I so messed up the project; I'm such a loser" or "What an idiot, they can't even follow the &%#@ directions."

Note: In TA, this is another example of the child voice speaking.

9   **Personalization.** The person sees themself as the cause of some negative external event that really had little or nothing to do with them.

10   **Deflection.** The person is unable to accept responsibility and immediately discounts or discredits those who disagree. For example, "Of course dinner was burned, I don't think the oven thermometer is accurate and this recipe is obviously flawed. You are always so dramatic; it is not as burned as you are saying."

To the extent that you can identify distorted thinking patterns in yourself and others, you can work to expose faulty logic. People who repeatedly think in these ways often have self-image issues, so it may not be easy to stop them from these distortions. However, if you can, it will help the other person (or you) develop a stronger sense of self.

Working styles

Do you know how you prefer to work? Or, put in the language of social psychology: Where are your strengths?

- As a *fact finder*?

- As a *follow thru*?

- As a *quickstart*?

- As an *implementor*?

There is an online assessment that does a very good job of identifying your working styles. It is called the Kolbe A Index, and it's easily found by an Internet search. The Kolbe A Index measures the way people instinctively work on projects. It captures their method of operation and identifies ways they will be most productive.

Test results show how you score in four dimensions: fact finder, follow thru, quickstart, or implementor. It is very helpful to know your own strength(s) and the strengths of those with whom you work closely. A *quickstart* might not be good at follow through. An *implementor* may not be comfortable thinking up new ideas or approaches. It stands to reason that when asking someone to help you with a task, it's useful to know how their working style meshes with you own.

At work, this information helps you choose the kinds of jobs that are most suitable for you and those you should probably avoid. In more intimate relationships, if the two (or more) of you take the test, you'll see how your various strengths are complementary or collide. We highly recommend it.

We are also big fans of an assessment tool called the *Myers-Briggs Type Indicator* (MBTI). It has helped us to understand our partner(s) and ourselves in ways that would not have occurred to us on our own.

According to their website (myersbriggs.org):

> The purpose of the Myers-Briggs Type Indicator (MTBI) personality inventory is to make the theory of psychological types described by C. G. Jung understandable and useful in people's lives. The essence of the theory is that much seemingly random variation in our behavior is actually quite orderly and consistent, being due to basic differences in the ways individuals prefer to use their perception and judgment.

Perception involves becoming aware of things, people, happenings, or ideas. *Judgment* involves the ways we reach conclusions about what we perceived.

The Myers-Briggs model is based on the premise that if people differ systematically in what they perceive and in how they judge, then we should be able to predict their interests, reactions, values, motivations, and skills. It turns out they were right.

Ultimately, Isabella Myers and Peter Briggs described 16 distinctive *personality types* that result from combinations of the various possible judgment/perception preferences. Here are the variables:

- In dealing with social situations, prefers one-on-one engagements (I) over crowded parties (E).

- In managing information, deals with facts (S) or interprets and adds meaning (N).

- In dealing with decisions, looks at logic and consistency (T) or at the people and special circumstances (F).

- In dealing with outside world, prefers to get things decided and closed (J) or stays open to new information (P).

Once the test has revealed your preferred ways of interacting with the world, your personality type is expressed as a four-letter code. Mine (Veronica's), for example, is ENFP. Bob is INTJ. You can learn to adapt your communication strategies (and even the ways you approach someone) by learning about the interaction between both of your Myers-Briggs personality types. This gives you a **huge** advantage in crafting clear and effective communication. When we typed both our Myers-Briggs codes into an Internet search, the results eerily match our interactions and the way we live our lives.

We are impressed with the test's accuracy. It has given us insights that improved our communications and relationships with people in general—and specifically with those for whom we know their Myers-Briggs profile. The following books provide the keys to understanding yourself, getting along with others, and interactions at work:

- **Please Understand Me: Character and Temperament Types** by David Keirsey and Marilyn Bates.

- **Please Understand Me II: Temperament Character Intelligence** by David Keirsey.

- **Type Talk at Work: How the Sixteen Personality Types Determine Your Success on the Job** by Otto Groeger, with Janet M. Thuesen and Hile Rutledge.

We found this the least expensive way to get an outstanding personality analysis.

Upsets

Winston Churchill once commented, "A man is only as big as the things that make him angry." Interestingly, Thomas Haliburton (writing in *Forbes Magazine*) commented that, "When a man is wrong and won't admit it, he always gets angry."

In a general way, *upsets* tend to rise out of unmet expectations. When we open our eyes in the morning, most of us begin processing the world around us and our experience of that world as positive or negative. We want every day to be a good day. We start gathering information to see if that expectation will be met. We tend to evaluate information that we receive from our senses as either good or bad. When we yawn and stretch as we get out of bed, we wince if we are sore and put that in the bad column. We listen to the weather report, and if it is going to be a rainy and cold day, we might put that in the bad column as well. As we add emotional charge to the information we are receiving, we color how we experience ongoing information. We might then stub our toe and decide, *This is going to be a bad day!*

Upsets occur at the intersection of expectations and disappointment. In life, we tend to have expectations about practically everything. For example, you expect your car to start in the morning. You expect illumination when you turn on a light switch. When something happens that differs from your expectation, you immediately assess whether the unexpected result is better or worse than anticipated. In other words, was this a good or bad turn of events? If bad, then how bad? If it is bad enough, or if we have had too many bad events too close together, we may become upset.

As our brains decode events, it makes interpretations and assumptions and builds a story of what we think we saw or heard happen. Ah! We now have a memory of what happened!

However, there is only a slim chance the memory is objectively accurate. This is because when an event hits a person's filters and interpretations, these filters skew what they experienced. It becomes transformed into something different. This *something different* is now their version of reality. (By the way, wars have started from this kind of misinterpretation of events.)

The person whose body is attached to that brain reacts to their understanding of what happened. Depending upon how closely that person's brain was able to correctly interpret the event, their response is both reasonable and logical, or rather misses the mark.

Some couples experience upsets with nearly every verbal exchange. Each person is processing what the other is saying and doing so through their own skewed perspective. This can result in misinterpreting the words or intent of the other. The result can lead to an upset. These snafus have to be addressed or they become part of the relationship's downward spiral.

As Mark Twain remarked, "Temper is what gets most of us into trouble. Pride is what keeps us there." How you handle upsets speaks volumes about your personal self-control. This section is designed to give you some options when you encounter situations that stir you up.

Stress

Stress often leads to upsets. In the same way that people handle upsets differently, they also process stress differently. You may not process stress the way your partner does. You are probably going to think your partner doesn't care when you are awake at night worrying about a relationship issue while you're watching them sleep like a baby. It is unlikely your partner doesn't care; it is more likely stress doesn't cause them sleepless nights.

Stress analysis is rather like threat analysis. First, make sure you understand what's causing the stress. Second, assess the threat level. Third, determine whether you have the skills, knowledge, and ability to cope with the situation. The last step is to remove what you see as the stress point. However, people often misjudge the kind of threat they're facing or their own abilities to address it.

Mark Leary, in "The Great Courses" audiobook *Understanding the Mysteries of Human Behavior* observed that there are four points where one person might experience more or less stress then another person:

1   Some people are exposed to more stressful events than others.

2   Some people judge events as more threatening than others.

3   Some people don't think that they can cope well with stress.

4   Some people try to cope with stress in ineffective ways.

When our coping mechanisms fail, we often become upset.

Being upset vs. having an upset

In 1975, I (Bob) went through a training course called *est*. That stood for Erhard Seminars Training, and it still exists as The Landmark Education Forum. There, I learned an important distinction. *Being upset* is conceptually different from *having an upset*. They pointed out that the phrase *I am upset* describes yourself as being that emotion, whereas *I am having an upset* is simply experiencing it. Once you have acknowledged you are *feeling* this (and not *being* this), you can recognize that emotions are transitory.

You are feeling this thing; you are not this thing.

In cases of extreme upset, you may be at the mercy of the upset; your emotions have run off with you. In a sense, your rational self has been hijacked. There are consequences for losing control of your emotional self. Those around you may change their opinion of you when they realize you have lost your self-control. In our culture, lack of personal control is viewed as a negative. You may be perceived as weak, volatile, bristly, or even dangerous.

> All of our anger and frustration is self-induced. The world might invite us to be upset, but we choose to accept the invitation.
>
> —Unknown

Stopping upsets

Tom Miller, in his course *Self-Discipline and Emotional Control*, observes that when someone is upset, they have surrendered control over their rational mind to their lizard mind (the part of your mind that reacts before you get a chance to filter your action). In this state, they no longer have full use of the defenses they have cultivated during their entire lifetime.

As adults, we have developed patterns to cope with specific things that come up in our lives. If A happens, we use our counter-A response. When B happens, we use our counter-B response. Such reactions are often automatic; they may seem beyond our control.

These ingrained responses probably helped you in the past, but may not be as helpful now.

Pattern interrupts represent one strategy to slow or stop ineffective or undesirable responses. This is a concept from NLP (neuro-linguistic programming). For example, the moment you sense you are getting upset, angry, or frustrated, take steps to change your emotional state. Stand up. Sit down. Stretch. Take deep breaths. Go get a drink of water. *Do* something different than what you've been doing. Change your physical position. This gives you time to get control over your emotional state. If you can stop the process of becoming upset and get control of yourself, you can then learn to **choose** your reaction. This isn't an overnight fix, but it suggests a way of choosing to behave differently than you have in the past.

Translation: Choose to *have an upset* rather than to *be upset*.

This is something like choosing to *have* ice cream. In the same way you can choose to have chocolate ice cream (to be upset), you could also choose to have vanilla ice cream (to have an upset). It's up to you.

Hint: Just before you are about to explode, you may sense some physical sensation in your body. In my (Bob's) case, the back of my scalp starts to tingle. This provides only a second or two before my lizard brain leaps into action. A second or two is *plenty* of time to change my emotional state. This works as long as you are prepared for the signs and have a plan about what to do when it occurs. It will take practice to develop new response patterns. This is not an easy task.

We suggest you explore a variety of ways to break your unwanted action–reaction cycles. Your goal is to turn them into an action–action cycles. You are responsible both for your actions and reactions. This applies equally to your partner.

Personally, we both use the distance method for assessing our reactions to unwanted situations. We ask ourselves, *What, exactly, am I upset about? How much does this truly matter to me now? Will I remember it (and will it still matter) in a week/month/year?*

For example, I (Bob) once had a partner who forgot to take the trash can to the street on trash day. In the morning, as I heard the trucks pull away from our house, I had a flash of anger. However, I quickly recognized that this was going to be an inconvenience, not a catastrophe. I also recognized that I was not likely to remember this incident in three months, let alone three years. So, no, it isn't worth having an upset about everything that goes awry in your life. Anyway, we usually forget the causes of small upsets; we just remember there was some kind of hiccup.

A word of caution: The process of moving from being upset to having an upset is a personal choice. We advise against trying to "teach" your communication partner how to defuse their upset when they are in the middle of one.

Managing upsets

Okay: Your partner/colleague is experiencing strong emotional reactions to something. Clearly, they are upset. It doesn't seem trivial. They aren't regaining composure quickly.

Most people would be concerned about the triggered person. They would start thinking things such as, *Wow, they must be under a lot of* stress, *This isn't like them*, or *I wonder if I should offer to help in some way*. Most people express compassion when someone is distressed.

Now imagine yourself as the person who had the outburst. You might feel embarrassed, ashamed, or remorseful. Self-recrimination can last much, much longer than the actual incident. We tend to be much more compassionate with others than with ourselves.

What's a possible first step toward recovery? How can we move past the negative, self-abusing patter that is going on in our heads? How do we learn from this?

One option, of course, is to tap into your compassionate side. One way to do that is to place this incident back into perspective. We tend to magnify upsets. Sometimes it helps to remember where you are and what you have to be grateful for.

The question is: How bad is it, really?

Really, you are in a First World country. You probably have adequate housing and food, you're safe from predators, you have running water, indoor plumbing, and a way of getting around the city and country. Statistically, you're in a very small percentage of the world population. According to the United Nations Development Programme's *Human Development Report* of July 2014, 50% of the world's population (7.7 billion people as of 2020) live on less than $2.50 per day, and 80% live on less than $10 a day. Twenty-two thousand children die daily as a direct result of poverty. Something like one in nine people worldwide do not have access to safe, clean drinking water. It's pretty sobering.

Next time you and your partner feel that your problems are almost insurmountable, you might reflect on those numbers. See whether it helps you put your issues into perspective. Hug one another. Go out for a cup of coffee—that costs more than half what the world's population makes in an entire day. You might also spend a moment or two finding reasons to be grateful and appreciate what is right in your life rather than concentrate solely on what isn't. Shift from needing to change what's wrong to having opportunities to improve.

When an upset includes others, there are some strategies you can use to improve the overall outcome:

- Acknowledge and validate their emotional state. For example, "It makes sense that you feel this way."

- Demonstrate curiosity instead of asserting they are wrong. Use this as an opportunity to get to know one another better. For example, "What just happened? What led up to this upset?"

- Anticipate a positive outcome. Train yourselves to feel positive rather than defensive. For example, "I know we can get through this together."

- Empathize with their experience. For example, "I understand how you are feeling, x makes me feel the same way."

- Be willing to change your own behavior rather than blame them. For example, "I apologize that something I said upset you. Can we speak about this so I can be more sensitive to your needs in the future?"

- Offer to support them as they process and resolve the conflict. For example, "Is there anything I can do to help?"

- Show appreciation rather than criticism. For example, "I see now how much this has upset you. I appreciate your willingness to express your emotions in front of me."

False memories

Like historians and novelists, we construe our own histories as we experience them. Our version of past events creates our current version of reality. Here is how it works.

Something happens. We simultaneously assess and interpret that event. We assign meaning to it, categorize its importance, and draw conclusions. We identify our responses: What we will do and what we will not do about it. We then form lingering opinions. This melding (or collapse) between *what happened* and the *meaning we assign to it* occurs in an instant. Objective memory of what really happened slips away. We are left only with our reconstruction of what happened as experienced through the distorted lens of our flawed perspective.

Interestingly, our capacity to remember something in its entirety as good or bad can actually be manipulated. Ample social-psychological research demonstrates that what happens at the very beginning, somewhere around the middle, and at very end of a conversation or event colors one's memory of the entire event.

For example, this three-part formula ensures the Super Bowl gets maximum income from advertisers. Viewers are on pins and needles at the start of the game; advertisements bracket the explosive halftime show; viewers are again swept up in their emotions at the game's outcome. Result: Viewers attach tremendous positive emotions to the advertisements.

The subjective versions of our own lifetime of experiences becomes the stuff and story of our lives. To a great extent, the kind of story you tell yourself depends upon the way you view yourself. Your view of yourself colors the way you view the world around you just as much as the way you interpret information moment-by-moment.

For example, people who view themselves as victims are sensitive to situations that validate their viewpoint.

This brings us to what we might call the downside of our stories: Our interpretations keep us in a loop. Without thought, we overlay our stories (or biases) onto current events. This puts a spin on almost everything that happens to us. Our stories represent the richness of what it means to be human. There is a power, validity, and value in them. However, you'll want to keep your background stories from spoiling your present life. It's important to find a balance between the voice of experience (the past) and being present in the here-and-now.

Regardless of how clever we are or how different we believe our circumstances to be, what continually emerges is pretty much what we believe about ourselves and the world around us. How many times have we thought, *Wow! How am I back in this situation again?* Easy: Our beliefs become our self-fulfilling prophesies. We've created our own recurring loop.

History is largely subjective. Particularly, your own version of your own history is largely subjective.

Apologies

While we are taking a look at ways to communicate so your partner feels heard and acknowledged, let's take a look at the fine art of apologies. What makes an apology effective? Great question; we are glad you asked. A good apology should not be about just getting off the hook. An apology is offered when we have wronged another. It is about beginning to heal the damage caused by the wrongdoing. To feel meaningful and heartfelt to the listener, it helps to know their language of apology.

Apologies, like gift giving, must be designed with the receiver in mind. Different people need different kinds of apologies.

According to Gary Chapman and Jennifer Thomas in their book *The Five Languages of Apology: How to Experience Healing in All Your Relationships*, there are five languages of apology:

1   Expressing regret

2   Accepting responsibility

3   Making restitution

4   Genuinely repenting

5   Requesting forgiveness

This is a four-step template we recommend when you have egregiously wronged someone and don't know their preferred apology preference (it incorporates the five Chapman/Thomas points):

1   **A clear statement of apology.** "Susan, I should have met you for dinner as I said I would. I apologize for being an hour late. I have no excuse for not doing what I said I would do."

2   **Expression of remorse and responsibility.** "I knew I had to leave work by 5 PM to get there in time. Instead of setting a timer, I just carelessly thought I could mentally keep up with the time. That was thoughtless and inconsiderate of you and damaging to our friendship. I sincerely regret taking advantage of you in such a way."

3   **A description how your actions (or lack thereof) impacted them.** "I know it could not have felt good to wait for me to show up and not even be able to be seated since the restaurant doesn't seat incomplete parties. I would have been embarrassed to wait that

long without someone arriving and it was wrong of me to put you through that. Our relationship is based on trust and I broke that trust by not showing up as I promised I would. I have damaged your ability to trust me as well as our friendship with my actions."

4   **A request for forgiveness that offers the possibility for making amends.** "Your friendship means more to me than my actions have shown you. I hope you can find it in your heart to forgive me at some point. I would like to take you to dinner on me in the hopes that I can start to rebuild the trust. Perhaps I could contact you the evening before any future scheduled meetings to confirm that I will be there and I could call or text you an hour before it's time to meet to reassure you that I am coming until you feel you can trust me again?"

Some people bristle at some types of apologies. As I (Veronica) have taught this topic over the years, I have found that some people are more interested in knowing it won't happen again than in hearing an apology. In such cases, consider explaining the steps you will take in the future to prevent reoccurrence.

Red flags

Bob and I are both *glass-half-full* kinds of people. We wrote this book to help others avoid painful blunders and missteps we have experienced in our own lives. Our blunders and missteps have caused us to become passionate about good and effective communication.

For the most part, you are dealing with others who have good intentions. However, not all people are actually okay. Not all people will speak with you in any sort of meaningful way. Also, people who know they are not okay may be able to mask their not-okayness for a time. Predators, for example, study ways to disguise their intent.

> While *most* people are sane *most of the time*, you may sometimes run across people where you aren't quite sure.

No doubt: You can still speak with someone who is not very nice. You simply have to be more careful with your listening and speaking skills. Watch for their reactions to what you say. Carefully read their facial expressions.

This section is intended to provide additional tips and skills for identifying someone with whom you should be a bit more careful than with others. We call these *red flags*, and they are behavioral warning signs that something is not quite right. They are not specific to any gender, sexual orientation, or relationship structure. It is important to recognize red flags, particularly when you are beginning a new relationship.

Our strong message to you is this: Take your time in establishing new relationships, for it may take time for problematic behaviors to emerge. When you see these patterns, we suggest you slow down or even stop the relationship in order to assess your situation. Generally, the more of these behaviors you observe in a person (and the more often you see them and the quicker they emerge in a new relationship), the more you might be at risk for being emotionally or physically harmed by this person.

POTENTIALLY ALARMING BEHAVIORS

As we were researching communication issues, we ran across an exceptional blog post by a woman named Epiphany. She said that Saikiji Kitalpha from *Second Life* had created a particularly thorough list of questionable behavior and had said that anyone could reproduce it but please give the author credit. Saikiji, you did a great job! (What follows is only slightly edited.)

Before you read this, please recognize that while you may find some of these behaviors in most people, you won't find clusters of them in people who are psychologically and emotionally safe and stable.

A caution: Not all of us are born with neurotypical brain wiring. A substantial (and apparently growing) number of us (Bob included) fall somewhere on the autism spectrum and exhibit certain unusual social behaviors. You might wish to familiarize yourself with autism spectrum disorder traits, as many people exhibit unusual social behaviors that can be off-putting at best and alarming at worst.

Now, on to the red flag behaviors:

1   They try to isolate you:

- They try to limit your access to other people in your life—friends, family, and your established social community.

- They forbid contact with others or they undermine outside relationships or activities.

- They are negative and unsupportive of your other (established) relationships.

- They monitor your communications (emails, phone calls, chats).

- They want you to quit your job, give up your car or telephone, or control your finances.

- They demand to know where you've been and who you've been with—often in an accusatory manner.

- They often call or visit unexpectedly.

- They become angry if you question them or if you show signs of independence or strength.

2   They are deceptive:

- They are reluctant to provide personal and factual information about themselves.

- They decline to give (or are dishonest about) their marital status when asked.

- They give inconsistent or conflicting information or details about themselves or past events.

- They have very limited times or places where you are able to contact them and they get angry if you try to make contact outside of those conditions.

- They do not give you their home or work phone numbers at the appropriate time.

- They have multiple online identities for interacting within the same groups.

- They cheat on you.

- They give the impression of being very successful without any evidence of real success.

- They disappear from communication for days or weeks at a time without explanation.

- They are evasive about their activities and plans, especially any unexplained absences.

- They rarely engage in normal, everyday conversations.

3   They behave oddly:

- Your friends warn you against them.

- They are critical of the company you keep and won't go to parties where most of the guests are friends of yours.

- They have no apparent references or friends you can talk to.

- They become angry, change the topic, answer questions with questions, or end the conversation when you ask personal questions or ask for references.

- They give you names of friends, but you can't verify that they even exist.

- They won't introduce you to their friends or family.

- They have a bad or no relationship with their family.

4   They seem insecure:

- They often exaggerate.

- They deflect blame to others for things going wrong

- They resort to extreme measures to prove that they, themselves, are not at fault.

- They do not take personal responsibility when things go badly and will not acknowledge their own mistakes.

- Their apologies feel insincere, phony, or are insulting.

- They put you down in front of others.

- They are constantly comparing themselves to others.

- They brag excessively about their experience.

- They engage in name-dropping.

- They avoid discussing what your possible future relationship could be like and tries to keep you in the dark about what might happen next.

- They appear to hide their vulnerabilities or behave in an emotionless manner.

- They hide behind their authority and demand that their authority not be questioned.

5 They are disrespectful:

- They do not respect your feelings, rights, or opinions.

- They are rude to public servers such as waitresses, cashiers, and janitors.

- They display little concern or awareness of the feelings or needs of others.

- They never or seldom says *Thank you*, *Excuse me*, or *I'm sorry*.

- They exhibit obvious and excessive displays of impatience.

- They believe that they deserve some particular reward or benefit, even at the expense of others.

6 They are manipulative:

- They try to make you feel guilty for not being "good enough".

- They belittle your ideas.

- They blame you for your hurt feelings.

- They blame you for their anger outbursts.

- They blame you for all relationship problems.

- They threaten to withdraw their love or leave you if you do not do as they wish.

7 They are inconsistent:

- They break their promises.

- They make plans with you, then make excuses for changing those plans.

- They treat you lovingly and respectfully one day and then harshly and accusingly the next.

- They go through extreme highs (behaving with great kindness) and pronounced lows (behaving with cruelty), almost as though they are two distinctly different people.

8   They are domineering:

- They pressure you into doing things you do not want to do.

- They do not respect your limits and won't negotiate; they want the relationship only on their terms.

- They push you too quickly into a personal relationship.

- They push you too quicky into a sexual relationship.

- They are overly demanding of your time and must be the center of your attention.

9   They are intemperate:

- They spend money largely and inappropriately on luxury items.

- They abuse alcohol or other drugs.

- They gamble excessively.

- They constantly ask for money or material goods from you or others.

- They fall in love with you way too fast or swear undying love before even meeting you.

- They begin expressing emotional neediness.

- They do or say things that result in getting themselves hurt.

10   They are temperamental:

- They lose control of their emotions in arguments; they raise their voice, calls you names, or blames you for things they did.

- They use force or violence to solve problems.

- They punch walls or throw things when upset.

- They turn on their peers, going quickly from *best friend* to *archenemy*, often for trivial or imagined reasons.

- They speak ill of others, particularly of people with whom they once were good friends.

- They display a disproportionately negative reaction to being told *no*.

- They hold excessive grudges against others and go to great lengths to get revenge on people.

- They threaten suicide or other forms of self-harm.

- They are hypersensitive and easily upset by annoyances that are part of daily life.

11   They have certain established behaviors or histories:

- They, themselves, were victims of abuse.

- They exhibit cruel behavior towards animals.

- They admit to hitting a partner in the past, but claim the partner made them do it.

Quite a list! It brings us neatly to the next chapter.

SEVEN GOOD HABITS FOR COMMUNICATION SUCCESS

1   **Be a bright light.** Go out of your way to spread lightness and hap-
    piness. Avoid speaking ill of anyone.

2   **Listen in neutral.** Listen to what others say without judgments.
    Avoid getting caught up in their stories (their version of events).

3   **Know who you are.** Understand your own standards and respect
    that others live by different standards. Neither are any better or
    worse than the other. Our daily behavior expresses our unique
    interpretations of our experiences. When people with widely
    different backgrounds are speaking, the door to miscommuni-
    cation is opened.

4   **Be outwardly optimistic.** Look at the glass as half-full. Con-
    centrate on looking for the good in all people and situations,
    regardless of how you may actually feel.

5   **Be proactive.** When you see something amiss, step up and par-
    ticipate. Be the example others follow.

6   **Take responsibility.** Own your role in repercussions resulting
    from your actions, whether large or small. Own your role in the
    situation. This is a core leadership characteristic.

7   **Check your facts.** Acknowledge that your opinions are not
    always facts. Be receptive to the idea that you sometimes remem-
    ber things in ways that favor the preservation of your self-image,
    and not because they are true.

Chapter 4
Issues and challenges

HARSH WORDS LEAVE WOUNDS; dishonesty breaks trust. In some cases, broken trust can never be fully restored. Once someone breaks your trust, every interaction with them is with someone you fundamentally distrust.

| Often, hurt people hurt people.

Whether in a work or personal setting, this loss of trust can create an escalating loop of unhappiness and discomfort. Depending on the depth of the wounding, one or both people may begin to disengage physically and emotionally.

Breach of trust affects people differently. You are likely to feel the betrayal more strongly when you are deeply involved in a relationship than if it occurred with a casual friend.

In fact, when it occurs outside of an emotionally connected relationship, breach of trust is less likely to be influenced by feelings of love, passion, friendship, or even respect. You may not be interested in fixing the situation. If the upset concerns a non-romantic friend, healing the wound(s) may enable you once again to become close. However, if you do not address a breach-of-trust issue with a partner, friend, or colleague, your stress may increase. Since built-up tensions affect your mental, physical, and spiritual self, it is often in your own best interest to resolve conflict—and release the emotional charge regardless of the type of relationship you have with that person.

The role of emotions in communication could easily become a book in its own right. To keep this project manageable, we have selected only four topics:

- Emotional issues

- Personal issues

- Financial issues

- Honesty issues

We chose these because they represent a range of emotional issues that influence your communication with others. Some of these ideas, tips, and techniques should help you work through challenging times that arise in work or personal relationships.

Emotional issues

Recent research suggests that the effects of stress differ for men and women. Researchers determined that males under stress tend to isolate more than women do. Also, men tend to be less able to distinguish their own emotions from those around them. Women under stress generally exhibit a different reaction. They become more pro-social. That is, they exhibit behavior that is positive, helpful, and intended to promote social acceptance and friendship.

In lay terms, this means that stressed men tend to withdraw, while stressed women tend to become nurturing. This bit of information is relevant for your communication style when stress is building up between you and someone else.

While there are lots of ways people respond to an emotional punch, common reactions include:

- **Punching back emotionally.** You raise your voice, raise the stakes, or begin threatening the other person.

- **Clamming up.** You won't talk about it right then and need to leave the room in order to process the situation privately. Perhaps you won't want to talk about it *ever*.

- **Dropping into stylized speech patterns.** You use clipped speech, flattened tonality, or repetition because you have been triggered into old emotional loops.

Your maturity in handling personal stress or pain (or the stress and pain that you cause another) is an important aspect of mastering your self-control as an adult. Clearly, it is also critical to maintain a stable relationship, whether at home or at work.

Perhaps the easiest way to approach emotional upsets is to develop emotional intelligence.

Emotional intelligence

In 1995, psychologist and science journalist Daniel Goleman published *Emotional Intelligence: Why It can Matter More Than IQ*. This work introduced the world to the emerging concept of emotional intelligence. His idea was that those who could manage their emotions could increase their success in life. This concept became popular and has continued to influence how we think about emotions and human behavior.

Justin Bariso (in his 2018 book *EQ Applied: The Real-World Guide to Emotional Intelligence*) took Goleman's ideas and identified actions that illustrate how emotional intelligence appears in the real world. Rewritten to match our writing style, these are the thirteen examples he developed:

1   **Think about your feelings.** Ask yourself questions about your own emotional strengths and weaknesses; consider how your mood affects your decisions; consider what might be going on with your emotions to have reacted as you did. Such internal work gives you an edge in work and personal relationships, as it helps build rapport with others (and understand when you have lost it).

2   **Pause.** Take time to hear what someone says before framing your reply. This keeps you from saying something in the heat of an emotional outburst that could have lasting impact.

3   **Control your reactions to events.** Listen in neutral. Avoid laying your judgments over what someone says or does. This frees you from being controlled by events, which makes it easier to live congruently with your own goals and values.

4   **Benefit from criticism.** Realize that criticism opens the door to learning—even if you didn't like the way the criticism was delivered. In this book, we recommend using the military model called an *after action review* (AAR) to process both the positives and negatives after performing a task or assignment. This also works well for processing criticism.

5   **Demonstrate authenticity.** Say what you mean, mean what you say, and stick to your values and principles. You *are* your word.

6   **Empathize.** Observe events in neutral and try to understand the thoughts and feelings of those involved with the event. This enables you to build better and more connected relationships.

7   **Praise others.** Be quick to point out the good in others (rather than judge others negatively). This inspires others.

8   **Give helpful feedback.** Be careful to provide only useful feedback. Negative comments about a person's work can be taken badly.

9   **Apologize when in the wrong.** Express your authenticity by taking personal responsibility for your role in an event that turned out badly. By the way, apologizing doesn't necessarily mean you were wrong, but it *does* mean you place higher regard upon a friendship than your own ego.

10 **Forgive and forget.** Life is short. To the extent you remain reactive to some real or imagined hurt, you distract yourself from being fully present. It's like having an open wound; you keep noticing it.

11 **Keep your commitments.** Your word is your bond. It becomes your character. Your character suffers when you fail to keep your word; your reputation strengthens as you develop a reputation for reliability and trustworthiness.

12 **Help others.** Much of what others think about you results from watching you help others. Such selflessness builds trust among those who know you and inspires others to follow your lead when the opportunity presents itself.

13 **Protect yourself from emotional sabotage.** Realize that some people take advantage of others by manipulating a person's emotions for their own benefit. As your own emotional intelligence increases, so does your protection from such people.

On the path to developing high emotional intelligence, there are some techniques concerning emotional self-control we'd like to share with you.

Emotional self-control

Stripped to the bare essentials, there are four components for handling your emotional upset.

STOP YOUR IMMEDIATE REACTION.

The first step in stopping heated emotional exchanges is to recognize how each of you are increasing or decreasing communication tension. Transactional analysis (ta) represents a fast and effective way to determine someone's emotional state. ta looks at verbal exchanges as transactions. Each transaction displays your respective ego states. Researchers identified three ego states: parent-like, child-like, or adult-like. These show up in speech, particularly during stressful conversations. You can understand quite a bit about someone's emotional state by paying attention to the words they use.

Because we discuss TA in Chapter Six, we will only mention now that it is within your power to switch from child–child or parent–child (self-perpetuating and emotion-laden upsets) to adult–adult discussions that help de-escalate the situation.

DISCONNECT FROM THE SITUATION

People seem to fall into one of three general camps:

1   Some people work through emotional issues when they arise.

2   Others specifically want to avoid continuing discussions over emotionally touchy topics until they can regain control of their own emotions.

3   Still others simply refuse to engage in any high-stakes emotional discussions at all.

We'll go over some solution-seeking strategies in the final chapter, including techniques you can use once you are ready to bring up the cause of the emotional conflict.

EXPLORE CAUSES

The military teaches soldiers to perform an AAR (after action review) whether or not a situation went well. It's a quality-management-and-control issue. While you can look up the military's format, the simplified civilian version is perfectly adequate:

- What happened?

- Did you like the outcome?

- Why did it happen this way?

- What needs to change so it does or doesn't happen this way again?

- What positive lessons came from the experience?

FLATTEN PRIOR ISSUES

When you fly, there is a difference between carry-on and checked luggage. This is also true when it comes to relationships.

When checked luggage is hauled out and opened, it can hold unpleasant surprises. Maybe your clothes have wrinkled, your shampoo bottle has leaked, or your favorite pocketknife has been confiscated.

While your partner is probably willing to help you with your carry-on luggage, they are likely not equipped to deal with any checked luggage that may be weighing you down. Unpleasant surprises seldom help a relationship. Solving these kinds of problems often require professional help.

By the way, you or your partner might have relationship baggage in addition to personal baggage. It's unfair to treat your current partner the way you learned to treat a prior partner. Here is another analogy, originally framed by Richard Moore during a personal conversation in 2015.

If you went into a restaurant and the waiter presented you with a bill just as you sat down, you would object. "This is not my bill! It's the last diner's bill!" you would say. "I know," the waiter would reply, "but the people at this table didn't pay their bill, so now it's yours if you want to eat at this restaurant."

You would get up and walk out. However, many of us stay in relationships where our partner is presenting us with unresolved "bills" from their past. It's not fair, but who said life was fair?

In this case, it's important to realize what you're dealing with and acknowledge why it may be hard to change someone else's reactions. They didn't settle their bill before beginning a relationship with you. They may not have even known about the bill, as their previous partner was the person who ran up the charges.

Keep in mind that people often speak or act assuming that their speech or actions are clear and obvious to others. That is not always so. You can use a stylized response structure to help reveal hidden messages (we discuss this more in the section titled "The Clarity of your Speech" in Chapter Five). The formula is this: *When you said (or did) X, I made that mean Y.*

Providing feedback that communicates how *you* understood what someone said or did fosters clear communication. When the person you're speaking with understands what you took their communication to mean, they know whether or not you heard what they intended to say. Sometimes the speaker's message or actions were unclear; other times the listener's baggage altered the intended message.

People have different levels of attachment to their life experiences. Some hold on to their past hurts because they are unsure what to do with themselves without these past hurts to explain why they are so stuck in life. Some people define themselves by their past; others, not so much.

Regardless of the way you manage your emotional history, your mental health depends on being able to stay in the present without being haunted by a past you cannot alter.

By the way, some issues are harder to flatten than others, especially if they involve broken trust. When *trust* is involved, you may want to explore the *Five Languages of Apology* that we mentioned in the previous chapter. The idea is, in order to begin healing, the hurt party needs to feel that the offending party actually feels remorse and wants to repair the damage.

Stuffing your feelings

Our discussion over the last few pages assumes that the two (or more) of you are embroiled in some passionate issue. However, some people *stuff* their views or opinions. They don't say them out loud. It's not emotionally healthy—but you knew that already.

People stuff their responses for many reasons. For example, someone might refrain from speaking out for fear it will escalate an already difficult situation. Another might withhold their thoughts because they are working or living in a system where their views are unwelcome. Yet another may not have ever learned to express their feelings, and instead developed passive-aggressive behaviors.

Whatever the reason, stuffing can be compared to Russian roulette. Everything seems fine until it isn't.

Emotional explosions frequently occur because underlying issues were not addressed when they first arose, possibly years earlier or in a prior relationship. When someone's response seems out of proportion to the triggering incident, it's probably not about you.

Typically, stuffing is a psychological self-defense mechanism. It may have started in childhood, adolescence, or even in adulthood. As a coping mechanism, it may have mostly succeeded for a while. However, emotional stuffing works against those attempting to establish and maintain a close and intimate bond with others. Yes, stuffing may avoid conflict, but it also prevents you from constructively working through the underlying issues.

As a general rule, there is a time and a place to express yourself. Balance is key. Waiting for an opportune moment is different than stuffing and is generally a wise course to follow.

Unconditional love

We believe that unconditional love exists. It does not require the loved person to do anything to earn that love. That being said, it is not the same thing as love without boundaries. You may love your partner but not like what they are doing right now. Unconditionally loving someone does not restrict you from building healthy boundaries. (By the way, expressing unconditional love for someone is a separate discussion from liking that person.)

Let's talk about this a bit. The phrase *unconditional love* expresses the conceptual opposite of *conditional love*—love that must be earned and maintained. With unconditional love, love is given freely to the loved one no matter what. Unconditional love endeavors to separate the behaviors and excuses of the loved one from any threat of loss-of-love due to bad behavior. For example, many parents continue to love a child who has become addicted to drugs.

Unconditional love has both a positive and a negative side.

On the positive side, showering someone with unconditional love supports them to become the person they want to be. It removes the burden that they must act or be a certain way to please others. Additionally, by distinguishing between love and behavior, you become open to the possibility of speaking with them about changing some of their behavior without invalidating them as an individual. This enables the other person to feel the emotional safety of knowing they are loved and valued, even when they make mistakes.

On the negative side, people sometimes think unconditional love means something that it doesn't. For example, people stay in abusive relationships because they say they believe in unconditional love, when—in reality—they are immersed in a relationship without healthy boundaries.

Unconditional love with boundaries is possible. For example, if the person you love unconditionally takes advantage of that love (or behaves in ways you find ethically or morally wrong), you may choose to love them in theory but not have them in your life.

Personal issues

Personal issues are barriers within yourself. These issues can cause you to snatch defeat from the jaws of victory. They are the parts of yourself that stand in your own way.

Obviously, all kinds of personal issues influence your communication skills and abilities. Some people have more common sense than others. Some people have had a more challenging childhood than others. In this section, we go over a few often-hidden topics.

We have divided this section into the following parts:

- Self-image

- Childhood hurts

- Jungian projection

- Orderliness vs. cleanliness

Self-image

Few people see themselves as others see them—a truism, to be sure. Even within your circle of friends, you know people who are emotionally stable and have high self-esteem, and you know people who live drama-filled lives and have low self-esteem.

I (Bob) once heard a (probably apocryphal) story of researchers who interviewed adult children of alcoholic parents. They conducted separate interviews of brothers who were three years apart in age. One of the men was an alcoholic; the other was not. Each man was asked about their drinking habits. One brother said, "I wouldn't touch the stuff, just look what it did to my parents." The other brother said, "Of course I'm a drunk. Who wouldn't be with parents like that!" Even people raised with very similar backgrounds draw quite different life lessons that affect their future. People develop different coping skills based on their self-image. Life lessons and self-image affect our ability to deal with our upbringing.

Obviously, your self-image is made up of lots of variables. Here are few to make sure we are on the same page:

- **Lovability.** Whether you see yourself as lovable or unlovable.

- **Ego sorting.** Whether you do or do not seek opportunities to help others.

- **Worth.** Whether you see yourself as worthy or unworthy.

- **Competence.** Whether you consider yourself generally effective or generally ineffective in most tasks.

- **Outlook.** Whether you approach life with the glass half-empty or half-full (or you expect someone else to fill it).

- **Validation.** Whether you consider a job well done because you completed it successfully or because someone else recognizes its success.

Childhood hurts

Humans are genetically predisposed to be on the lookout for bad things. We are designed to recognize and remember the bad, and build strategies from them. Researchers refer to this tendency towards caution as *negativity bias*. This bias leads us to focus more on bad things, making them seem more important than they are objectively. Negativity bias has been bred into us since prehistory. For millennia, life was so risky that only the careful survived.

Now let's consider personal memory. Bad things happened in all of our childhoods. Adults who were there may not have considered something to be bad, but our child-brains interpreted it that way. Because of this, we all developed strategies to deal with perceived threats. Most of those strategies were reasonable and logical; some not so much. To this day, you may have unexplainable reactions to certain events.

I (Veronica) was having a glorious time playing on the monkey bars with my friends as a five- or six-year-old child. My friends and I had the brilliant idea to place a very large cardboard appliance box under the monkey bars and jump into it. I managed to land with a leg on either side of a wall on that box. The box didn't budge. This was *extremely* painful and mortifying in front of my friends. That combination translated into my not ever again wanting to play on a playground. To this day, I still feel a bit embarrassed when I see a playground.

Defensive reactions developed in childhood often create behavior patterns that can be triggered as an adult. If you (or someone with whom you're speaking) reacts strongly to certain situations in surprising ways, chances are there are some buried defense mechanisms lingering about. The problem is, you're no longer in situations where those learned reactions are helpful. In fact, they may potentially harm you. Here are a few examples of ways childhood reactions can play out in adulthood.

First example: I (Veronica) knew someone who had an abusive mother. She developed a strong suspicion of all women. She felt women were untrustworthy, mercurial, and possibly dangerous. She spent most of her formative years and young adulthood avoiding making relationships with women. She treated women in positions of authority with suspicion at best and outright hostility at worst.

Second example: Some parents overemphasize the importance of being thin or fit. This emphasis may cause issues such as anorexia or bulimia nervosa. Current statistics indicate that nearly thirty million adults suffer from eating disorders and that approximately one person dies every hour from those conditions.

Common sense tells us that long-term relationships run smoothly when partners understand (and support) one another's motivations and dreams. In healthy relationships, each person shares their concerns and upsets in order to prevent little issues from growing into elephantine conflicts and misunderstandings. In that light, the person who hides knowledge from the other is inhibiting the relationship. More explicitly, the emotionally closed person (the person keeping secrets) restricts the relationship's growth by not matching their partner's level of emotional risk. The level that a person is willing to take emotional risk can often be tied to their childhood experiences.

Chances are, a situation like this won't last long. We are speaking from experience.

In business settings, we can hardly overemphasize how important it is for all team members to share information relevant to a project, task, or the company as a whole. In most contexts, sharing builds (reinforces) trust.

Jungian projection

This topic is well known; it's easy to find good information about it (for example, see jungstudies.net). The key concept is that people sometimes project their personal motives or insecurities onto those close to them and then react to what are, essentially, their own issues. This loop becomes visible when one person cannot understand why the other person is making a big deal out of something that was such a non-event.

For example, let's say that you have a pattern of leaving tasks incomplete. You are good at starting things, but you tend to lose interest before finishing them. It is a weakness in yourself that has bothered you for years.

You have asked someone else to do something. However, when you check in to see how they are doing, they are not as far along as you had expected. As a result, you jump to the conclusion that they are not going to complete the task, and this makes you reactive and upset. This is a response to how you feel about *your own* inability to complete tasks, projected onto the other person. You are reacting against yourself and have projected your own shame and feelings of inadequacy onto *them*. The other person doesn't understand any of this. They only know you have lashed out against them for doing what they thought you asked them to do.

Not all people solve the same problem in the same way. We're back to *the usual error.* That is, assuming others are like you.

This is bad enough, but it can get worse. These cycles often feed off themselves. For example, if your partner has abandonment issues (perhaps they come from a broken home, or had a spouse leave without notice), they might interpret some of your actions as signs you are considering ending the relationship.

As abandonment fears well up, reactions can vary from person to person. In their state of heightened sensitivity, they may become clingy, distant, suspicious, accusatory, etc. New and confusing messages sent by their partner can lead to new and different responses from the "accused party." These changes may, in turn, be interpreted as more signs that abandonment is imminent.

Landmines. Triggers. Big red flags. Unhappiness.

If the person concerned about being abandoned had simply mentioned their concerns directly with their partner, that partner may well have said, "What? I didn't do that because I'm thinking of leaving you, the actual reason is..."

Deeply embedded fears are often steeped in serious trauma. Transparent communication can help ease these fears. So can purposefully supportive behavior. That being said, many issues are not easily resolved and may require professional help.

Orderliness vs. cleanliness

I (Bob) am going to bring this up—briefly—as it's been a particular issue in my own life. With my high-functioning autism, I care more that the house is tidy and orderly than whether the carpets have been vacuumed or the kitchen floor mopped. Personally, an orderly house is a *need* and a clean house is a *want*. This can lead me to spend significant time tidying up in areas that are invisible to my partner.

I realize that high-functioning autism is an unusual condition, so few readers are going to resonate with this issue. However, people have all kinds of idiosyncrasies. Most of us are relatively normal; others of us are somewhat eccentric. In my opinion, relationships benefit from some in-depth discussions about personal preferences and where they fall on the *needs vs. wants* continuum.

Financial issues

Financial issues can cause friction and emotional trauma among couples. As we see it, this topic has five components. They are worth reviewing, as friction affects stress and stress affects clear communication:

1   Financial scarcity

2   Financial imbalance

3   Feeling trapped

4   Spending habits

5   Emergency provisions

Everyone gets stressed when you spend more than you make. Everyone reading this book knows the common answers. You can use a tightly controlled budget; you can start preparing to get a better paying job. Of course, one or both of you can start working a second job, but that might create additional friction over the scarcity of time you can spend together. This is certainly a challenge.

Financial scarcity

Many people find themselves without enough money to cover their basic expenses. This happens because the economy changes, because you lack education or training for advancement, or because of age or medical conditions. These are all familiar issues for which a variety of corrective options are available. You can take distance-learning courses, read and study more about your field, join networking groups, etc.

More importantly, you can change your mental relationship with the concept of money and wealth. This path is well described by people writing about the *Law of Attraction*. (You might start with the book *What to Say When You Talk to Yourself* by Shad Helmstetter that we mentioned in Chapter One. It will show you how to start the change process from the inside out.)

Financial imbalance

In some relationships, one person essentially surrenders financial control to the other. Sometimes that works out well; sometimes it doesn't.

There is a palpable fear of letting go of one's financial safety net. We get it. This can be particularly true when one person has far more assets than the other. How does it work if one of you is worth, say, half a mil and the other person is living paycheck-to-paycheck? If one person has a long history of financial management and the other has none? Here, we highlight areas that may underlie some hidden concerns, fears, or anxieties that can affect your ability to communicate cleanly with your partner.

People who have grown up far above or far below the average U.S. norm probably exhibit behaviors that, while invisible to themselves, stand out to people with more average upbringing. Despite best intentions, these differences can make others uncomfortable.

For example, some people who have grown up amidst wealth may (subtly) assume they are entitled to special or preferential treatment. Likewise, others (particularly those with substantial education or business backgrounds) may assume they are naturally better prepared to lead a relationship (or conversation) and are intolerant of opposing viewpoints. Most people tend to notice those who have grown up with what is euphemistically called *entitlement*. If you find yourself thinking, *She acts like such a snob* or *He's so condescending*, you've just experienced someone expressing an attitude of entitlement.

When there is a large asset gap between people, it can cause the person with the greater assets to speak and act differently than if the assets or incomes were more closely balanced. I (Bob) know one couple where the man had no assets to speak of (and a very modest income) while the woman had substantial wealth and didn't work because of her outside income. She handled all financial decisions—usually without consultation. After some years, the man found himself in a new job. He now earned enough to support the family. His wife commented to me that he announced on the day he took that job that he now intended to be much more involved with financial decisions and budget control. I silently noted that their financial imbalance must have been an unrecognized stress point that he had never been willing to discuss.

Feeling trapped

Almost regardless of income, many people feel financially trapped in their relationship. After all, it often takes both people's incomes and assets to support the lifestyle to which they have become accustomed. The dynamic often changes when one person realizes they are financially entangled and without the ability to live on their own. For example, they may start tolerating a lot of bad behavior from the other person.

Personally, we recommend establishing individual dedicated savings accounts to hold six months of living expenses plus moving and resettlement costs.

Financial independence goes a long way towards giving you a voice in any discussion. You won't fear the consequences of speaking truth at work or at home.

Spending habits

Friction can develop when one person can dip into their independent assets to buy pretty much whatever they want. Imbalance within a partnership (whether work or domestic) speaks to the difference between each person's values and beliefs. People with similar values and beliefs are likely to be able to build a smooth relationship.

If money is a hot topic in your relationship, you might want to plan ways to manage the discussion. For example, the two of you might want to explore each of your beliefs about money and what it symbolizes (freedom, security, etc.). Develop shared plans for events such as one of you losing their job.

Emergency provisions

The very act of discussing contingency plans provides an opportunity to raise personally important issues. The way discussions develop can affirm or threaten trust between partners. On the positive side, financial and emotional candor can help to ease abandonment fears by demonstrating trust. You can help drive off the dragons of imagination by planning for a variety of financial, medical, and relationship crises. This is particularly true for aging couples who might be facing complicated medical issues.

Emergencies bring stress. Preparation eases stress. At a bare minimum, consider writing down information about where to find key medical, financial, and insurance information.

Surprises happen. Case in point: In 2006, I (Bob) had a nearly fatal heart attack. It was a week after moving in with a former partner. Nothing was in place for emergencies. I arrived at the hospital and without so much as my medications list. I learned a lot from that experience. My meds list now has a permanent home in my wallet, and my partner has access to my current passwords. I've prepared a document titled *If I am dead or hospitalized* and placed it as the first file in the "My Documents" folder on my computer. On my cellphone, my home screen is blank except for a single *notes* icon. Opening that icon directs you to the emergency instructions on my computer.

It is pretty easy to prepare for "normal accidents." The key is to work with someone you trust to document important areas of your life. In general, this includes:

- Setting up your cellphone to help first responders know whom to call if you cannot speak.

- Keeping a list of medications and other important medical information on you (such as in your wallet or on your phone).

- Putting aside emergency funds and ensuring you (and someone you trust, if you so choose) have easy access to that money (whether it is cash or in a bank account).

- Establishing powers of attorney for medical necessity.

- Documenting DNR (do not resuscitate) orders as part of a living will.

- Establishing a personal representative to handle your affairs at various points, including in case of death.

Note: We have included a list titled "Preparing for Normal Accidents" in the *Supplementary Material* at the end of this book.

Honesty issues

It can be scary to be honest. It can be a relief to be honest. It can hurt to be honest.

But what does *honesty* mean? Our guess is that it doesn't mean exactly the same thing to your business partner (or your relationship partner) as it means to you. One challenge about honesty is that people have differing views about whether divulging (or not divulging) information is dishonest. For many, honesty can be influenced by the particular set of circumstances occurring at that particular time. People who endorse *situational honesty* believe that outcomes—rather than set rules of behavior—justify the way you do things.

Nonetheless, honesty has boundaries and limits that have evolved from your values. As we have already discussed, your values developed from your upbringing, experiences, and education. As with many things in life, honesty has some subjective qualities to it.

When a work colleague asks "Hi, how are you today?" they don't want an answer that requires real interaction. Actually, they usually don't want to hear anything negative.

When your domestic partner asks "How was your day?" they certainly don't expect you to take the next eight hours to provide a minute-by-minute recital.

So: How much honesty do you want from your co-worker or your partner, and vice versa? Some people want lots of details; others, not so much.

You have to develop your own acceptable limits and expectations about honesty as it relates to integrity and trust. If you're seeking harmony in your relationships, your partners have to understand (and agree) with your limits.

But that's theory, and now we'll get down to practice.

Personal honesty and integrity thrive when people have a solid and happy relationship based on mutual respect. These qualities thrive when both people feel that life with their domestic partner (or their work partners) is interesting and personally fulfilling.

When something changes in the dynamic and those warm fuzzy feelings start to go away, there is a human tendency to put up walls of emotional protection. If one person starts to question the other person's commitment to the relationship, red flags of warning start to unfurl. Remember what we said very early in this book: If you're not *working* on your relationship, you're not *in* the relationship. People can tell when their partner isn't as committed to the relationship as they were before.

Trouble *really* starts if one person's *wants* are being met at the sacrifice of their partner's actual physical, medical, or psychological *needs*.

There are three areas where honesty comes up:

1   Omission and commission

2   Lying

3   Willful opposition

Omission and commission

Let's go a bit further with the *situational honesty* topic.

In work or in personal relationships, most people view omission and commission equally as trust violations. The difference between an act of *omission* and an act of *commission* is the difference between withholding the truth about something vs. voicing a lie. Acts of omission and commission are ethical issues.

One of my (Bob) former partners put it this way:

> Imagine *trust* as a fresh sheet of paper. Think of *broken trust* as that piece of paper being crumpled. Even if you iron the crumpled paper, it will never again look new. Your word is your bond and it is all you have in this world; be careful how you pledge your word.

In our view, you have daily opportunities to practice living up to your word: being places when you say you'll be there. The more you are able to keep your word on small issues, the more you'll find it easy to keep your word on large issues. You will have developed the habit of being reliable.

Acts of omission or commission can be grounds for ending a relationship. If it's serious enough, one single act may separate a couple, even after many years together. For example, we have a friend whose wife of 28 years filed for divorce the moment she discovered he'd had a one-night stand. You may know couples where something like this has happened.

Lying

There is science surrounding the concept of lying. Pamela Meyer has done quite a bit of work in this field. She also has a TED talk on this topic. She has presented some really interesting information. Here are a few takeaways from her material:

- People lie to you from 10 to 200 times a day.

- When you first meet someone, chances are they will lie to you three times within the first ten minutes.

- Extroverts lie more than introverts.

- Women generally lie to protect other people.

- Married couples lie to one another about 1 in 10 interactions.

- Unmarried couples lie to one another about 1 in 3 interactions.

We are surrounded by lies, yet not everything that is honest needs to be said.

We have all met people who proclaim, "Look; I'm just being hon-est!" when in fact, they know they are using their statement as an excuse to be hurtful. Often, the speaker uses the "brutally honest" defense to make aggressive and unwarranted critical comments. Some issues are more sensitive than others. We've all been taught social graces; we know there is a line between responding appropri-ately or inappropriately. The general rule is not to volunteer hurtful information just for the sake of being honest.

When it comes to honesty, I (Veronica) live by a code. I tell myself and others that I *try* to be honest. I make an earnest attempt every day not to lie. When I get stopped by a police officer and they ask me what I did, that goes out the window! I don't just say, "Well, officer, I was completely disregarding the speed limit and I was merrily going 15 miles over. I also tend to get out of tickets because I'm reasonably attractive and likeable. When I speed, I am betting that I am going to get out of a ticket if I get stopped." There is a line between *honesty* and *foolhardiness*. It actually pains me when I lie, because I've bro-ken a moral pact I have with myself.

Having said all that, living as we do in this day-and-age, it's sim-ply impossible to be 100% honest and also to maintain complex and close business and personal ties. We personally suggest that you cul-tivate and listen to your internal moral compass when navigating the complexities of your life. Consider taking a longer-term view of a situation or conversation. Will your supposedly-honest answer help or hurt the person with whom you are speaking (or yourself) in a month, a year, a decade? You can't unsay things.

Know this: The more you lie, the easier it gets.

Interestingly, the more we want something, the more we override our own critical thinking. The better we know the person speaking with us, the more we will believe them. The friendlier someone appears, the more susceptible we are to their persuasion. This is why we keep getting suckered into paying more for something than we intended; it is why we purchase things we know we didn't really want or need.

Meyer goes on to explain that our culture sanctions lying—it's hereditary: "Babies will fake a cry, pause, wait to see what happens, then go right back to crying."

If this topic interests you, here are some books we particularly like:

- **Never Be Lied to Again: How to Get the Truth in 5 Minutes or Less in Any Conversation or Situation** by David J. Lieberman.

- **What Every BODY is Saying: An Ex-FBI Agent's Guide to Speed-Reading People** by Joe Navarro with Marvin Karlins.

- **Read 'Em and Reap: A Career FBI Agent's Guide to Decoding Poker Tells** by Joe Navarro with Marvin Karlins.

- **Liespotting: Proven Techniques to Detect Deception** by Pamela Meyer.

In current times, we are living in what is frequently referred to as a "post-truth society." Increasingly, people accept an argument based on emotions and personal beliefs rather than on verifiable facts. That is, lying has become widespread.

Think about the implications of widespread lying in terms of our current Internet age, where we are constantly assaulted by information of all kinds. We pick up our phones and unverified information is spoon-fed to us. Unfortunately, we contribute to the "post-truth" culture by sharing misleading (or wholly inaccurate) information, as we promote our own social media to become more popular (rather than telling the truth).

Social media is rife with:

- Spam

- Trolls

- Catfish

- Fake news

- False intimacy

- Identity thieves

- Ponzi schemers

In fact, the world-famous astrophysicist Neil deGrasse Tyson offered the very best summary of this situation we have ever heard. In the opening lines of his "MasterClass" (youtube.com/watch?v=Jc3du7i-9EMw) he observed, "One of the great challenges in this world is knowing enough about a subject to think you are right, but not knowing enough about the subject to know you are wrong."

Everyone can be deceived about something they desire. So the question becomes, how can you spot a liar? Let's spend some time learning how to tell when someone is lying to you. (This applies to a non-professional liar. Someone who lies for a living won't be easy to spot—they know how to overcome these tells.)

There is an art to reading body language. We have summarized a few common observations that professional investigators use to help them assess a suspect's truthfulness. Bear in mind, these guidelines apply to amateur liars, not professionals. People who depend upon

dishonesty for their livelihood know all about this and have prac-
ticed how not to give these signals. (Obviously, this is very short list
adapted from the books we cited. They are wonderfully interesting
books and we urge you to pick up copies if this area interests you.)

Here are a few *tells* that someone is lying to you:

- **Unusual body movements.** Body language (and often breathing
  pattern) will change slightly when a normally truthful person
  starts telling a lie. Their breathing may get deeper and louder.
  You may see unusual or oddly timed posture shifts. In some
  cases, their body will start looking defensive: arms crossed,
  legs crossed, shoulders pulled up, and elbows pulled more into
  their sides.

- **Hand movements.** When amateur liars say something they
  know is not true, they may express discomfort through hand
  movements. They may clench their fists to keep their hands
  from moving or (at the other extreme) fidget a lot with their
  hands while speaking.

- **Voice pitch.** Vocal pitch tends to go up when lying. This happens because the tension involved with lying tightens our
  muscles. When larynx muscles tighten, they produce a higher
  pitched sound.

- **Covering their mouth or face.** Sometimes, even intentional liars
  forget to monitor these nearly-instinctual behaviors. Suppos-
  edly, this happens because their subconscious mind wants to
  avoid telling the lie, and covering part of their face represents
  symbolically hiding.

- **Unusual pauses or delays in responses.** Watch for unusual
  breaks in a conversation when someone is speaking with you. A
  liar may hesitate as they work on creating their deceptive story.

Willful opposition

If one person in a relationship is willfully opposing the other, they are sending a message. You'll want to open that message and understand it. Personally, we would say that you do not have the luxury of ignoring it. You need to know what's going on (unless, of course, you've already decided the relationship is over).

One reason you want to find out what's going on is that *nothing* may be going on. You may be imagining the whole thing. Remember our discussion about *projection*? One of you may be misinterpreting the other's actions. That's why communication is so important.

Let us tease this apart for a moment.

People solve problems in ways that work for them but may not make much sense to those watching. I (Bob) have had to work closely with a few people whose working styles confused me and seriously increased my stress. In one particular case (a domestic partner, actually), I did not understand the way they arrived at their final product or solution. Their final solution was okay, I suppose, but it missed the mark for being my version of the best solution. Also, not all the tasks were completed. Task completion is very important to me, because when some tasks are unfinished, I have to go back and do them myself, or bring the problem back up with my partner. I was not a happy camper.

In the most general way, supervisory behavior falls into two categories: one approach takes the *macro* (large-scale, visionary) view of task management; the other takes the *micro* (small-scale, detailed) view.

When assigning a task, the macromanager expects the person completing it to devise their own approach. The micromanager expects that person to complete it according to a detailed predefined approach. Macromanagers focus on *getting* a job done; micromanagers focus on *how* the job gets done.

Here is an example of each management approach. You and a co-worker (or your partner) need to attend a meeting in a distant city over a specific weekend. As a *macromanager*, you may give broad parameters about dates, ticket costs, or the type of hotel, but basically, you just want the task completed. Beyond that, you leave the other person alone. They may or may not come to you a few times with clarifying questions. As a *micromanager*, assigning a task is always accompanied by a discussion of the important variables such as:

- Optimum ticket price given arrival and departure times

- Particular airports at each end (if relevant)

- Seat preferences

- Frequent flyer account numbers

- Hotel preferences (especially hotel club memberships)

- Special room requests (extra pillows or towels, room location)

- Proximity of the hotel (or the room) to meeting locations

- Rental car company to use (with club membership numbers)

- Weather check

- Dining or entertainment reservations plus addresses

- And so forth

Keep in mind, some tasks are more important to one person than to another. A macromanager might have explicit instructions for where they sit on a plane, and a micromanager may not care at all. The point we are making is that regardless of management style, you are trying to achieve the same result: a successful trip.

While constant micromanagement can wear you out and annoy your partner, it can be a useful tool to learn about their working and thinking styles. Close scrutiny can help establish (or re-establish) trust in their judgment. Often, micromanagement provides that information.

Why would I care about this detail? you ask. *The results should be the same.*

Yes, the results *should* be the same. But what if they aren't? This is really a communication exercise to determine how explicitly one person specifies a task and how well the other person executes it.

It's good news if the result turned out well (whether you used a macro or micromanagement approach). You have just had a demonstration that you can work well together.

If the experience did not turn out as you'd expected, you'll want to determine the cause of the stumble. Here are some common causes:

- You provided imprecise directions from the start (you might have glossed over important details or failed to explain the importance of certain sequences).

- Your partner had an imprecise understanding of those directions (they may have been inattentive, assumptive, or failed to ask clarifying questions).

- Your partner lacked the skills or knowledge to needed complete the task as you wished (they didn't know that they didn't know how to complete the task, so did not know what questions to ask in the beginning).

- Your partner messed it up willfully.

By the way, external factors can cause inattentiveness and will-fulness. It matters whether someone is on medication; it matters whether there are hormonal imbalances (yes, men too); it matters whether there are unusual stressors or illnesses. It could even matter whether one or more of you had a drink before starting a complex task. One drink can be sufficient to blunt someone's abilities; one drink may make some people hypercritical; one drink may make someone care less.

Given any of these conditions, it may be hard to tell whether the task went awry because the person was impaired, inattentive, or actively resisting a clearly stated preference.

The issue of discerning willfulness from inattentiveness, and what you do about it, is pretty important. The next chapter (on commu-nication theory) is designed to empower you to solve these kinds of challenges—ideally before they escalate.

SOME IDEAS ARE OBVIOUS...

Some ideas are obvious once you hear (or read) them:

- **The last three minutes.** Psychologists say that your most vivid memory of an encounter or event is strongly influenced by what happened in the last three minutes. In fact, it's been shown that you'll have a stronger recollection of that good or bad ending than you'll have of the overall occurrence. By extrapolation, it's *very* important to say loving and supportive things to your partner just as you're going to bed—or before you are going to be apart for a while. Similarly, you wouldn't want to end a workday by criticizing a work partner.

- **Communicate.** You can't expect to have what you want if nobody knows about it.

- **Create a *joy jar*.** Daily, each of you write down an example of how the other person made you joyful that day. Then, put these slips of paper into a jar. When you're feeling low, pull one or two out and read them. Re-experience the joy.

- **Complete difficult conversations.** You know it's true: If you do not want to say something, it should be expressed and discussed. Communication at this level stabilizes relationships. Closure confers respect for the relationship. Discussing something you don't want to (and know you must) enables you to kick one of the "elephants" out of the room.

- **Overcome negativity.** It's difficult to be happy with a negative worldview. You may react negatively to behaviors in others that you actually dislike about yourself, or based on subconscious assumptions about who is and is not "okay" in your world.

Chapter 5
Communication theory and technique

> "Most of the time we don't communicate, we just take turns talking."
>
> **—Anonymous**

COMMUNICATION IS CERTAINLY A well-discussed topic. There is a sea of books and articles on the subject. You might wonder why we would take the time to write a book on this subject, considering how well it's already covered.

Answer: This book synthesizes both obvious and often-overlooked information from many disciplines—sociology, psychology, business, management, etc.—and delivers manageable chunks of communication theory that both Veronica and I have found pragmatically useful in our lives.

Parts of this chapter are light (funny), and other parts are heavier (thought-provoking). Much like communication in general, this chapter can seem complex at the start, but gets easier as our techniques become part of your communication style.

The major sections are:

- Communication challenges

- Basic skills

- Being engaging

- Communication effectiveness

When upsets occur, we tend to use one of two tactics: we either *defend* or *convince*. When we defend, we deflect and diminish information that is contrary to our "rightness." When we convince, we just need to show the other person how they are wrong so they can see our "rightness."

A communication-misfire usually begins when someone is speaking from their own viewpoint, not considering (or has no way of knowing) the other person's. As a result, the speaker's messages are phrased in their own (rather than the listener's) language. Among other things, this means they have made assumptions about how much the listener knows or remembers about the topic being discussed.

Along these lines, communication hiccups also occur when the speaker uses imprecise words, forcing the listener to interpret the speaker's meaning. For example, someone might utter a sentence like this: "You know, like clean up your car and pick up some lunch." The listener might wonder: *Do they mean clean out the car's interior or do they mean wash the car? Do they want me to vacuum the inside of the car, too? Lunch... am I supposed to come back with my lunch? Am I getting lunch for them, too? And when am I expected back?*

As if this isn't enough, all kinds of distractions can contaminate the overall process. For example, even while speaking and listening, both people are simultaneously making judgments about each other, keeping track of other things going on around them, and wondering what they are going to have for dinner. This keeps people from being fully present. Bottom line: People remember verbal exchanges somewhat differently. You'd need a video of a conversation to unravel what really happened.

This chapter focuses on your own speaking and listening skills. How clearly you utter your message relies on two communication skills. The first concerns how correctly your reply matched what was said (how well *you* were listening). The second bears on how well you adapted your own word choices to the other person's listening characteristics. Once we have covered these areas, we will touch on *projection* before ending up with *upsets*.

Communication challenges

As John Stewart noted in *Bridges Not Walls: A Book About Interpersonal Communication*, "Interpersonal communication is a mutual relational, co-constructed process, as opposed to something that one person does to someone else."

Some communication succeeds; some fails. This is just a fact of daily life. Clearly, communication influences every aspect of any relationship. When people communicate, they define themselves. Also, they respond to their perceived definitions of others. However, since these perceptions are always subjective (and therefore inherently distorted), an attempt at communication often leads to misunderstandings and bad feelings—causing people to shut down.

This part of the book is intended to give you some basic communication theory. Ideally, it should clean up your outgoing messages and help you to better identify missing elements when someone is speaking with you.

Here is a made-up example of communication failure waiting to happen. One person says, "I want ham and cheese for lunch." The other person says, "Great, I want ham and cheese too." Superficially, you'd think they have a match. Maybe yes, maybe no. Is the first person asking for a croque monsieur? A simple ham and cheese sandwich? Perhaps a ham and cheese omelet? Conceivably, a slice of deli ham rolled in a slice of cheese?

How does the listener verify they understood the speaker? Sometimes it's not so easy. While the listener is likely to have understood the meaning of each word, they may well have missed the speaker's overall intent.

The phrase *communication challenges* suffers from the uncomfortable combination of two poorly defined words: **communication** and **challenges**.

Communication describes a process of transmitting and receiving an idea (or message) between sentient beings. It may involve speaking, using facial or body gestures, wearing certain clothing, etc. Right now, we want to use the word to refer to two or more people speaking.

As we have been saying throughout this book, at the most basic level, the way you speak is a result of:

- The specific situation

- Your history with those with whom you're speaking

- Your communication skill level (including your education and work experiences)

- Your emotional and physical state and the emotional and physical states of those around you

- The intention of your message (e.g. delivering facts, being romantic, managing a crisis, conveying emotion)

- Etc.

The way you speak is fundamentally influenced by whether you are speaking:

- With someone (two-way communication)

- At someone (one-way communication)

- To an audience (lecturing)

- With a brainstorming team (cooperative)

- To a supervisor (deferential)

- To a subordinate (authoritative)

- Etc.

In English, the word *communication* (or *communicating*) carries the connotation that the other person is in fact, understanding the messages you are sending. Communication is considered to be a back-and-forth process. Statements such as *I am communicating with [not at] Bill* or *We are in communication* signal a two-way flow of information.

On the other hand, the word *speaking* carries no such connotation. You could easily be speaking to your neighbor, and in reality, you are simply venting. You are not expecting interaction from a one-way communication. You can speak quite successfully to a brick wall.

Challenges can be an equally messy word; it carries multiple connotations in English. It can mean that you feel:

- Confronted (challenged) by some authority. For example, a uniformed officer yelling "Stop! Police!" while you're taking a walk.

- Confronted (challenged) with resistance. For example, your partner saying "I don't want to talk about it" when you ask about their day.

- Difficulty (challenged) conveying the message you're trying to send to a listener. For example, a colleague asking "Could you please explain that differently?" while you're giving a presentation to the team.

- Uncomfortable (challenged) stepping outside your comfort zone. For example, a friend suggesting "Let's try a new cuisine" despite knowing you're a picky eater.

- Traumatized (challenged) having a message conveyed to you by a speaker. For example, your significant other screaming "Your stupidity knows no bounds; how could you have possibly thought that I wanted x? Haven't you learned anything about me over the last three months?" when you offer them tea instead of coffee.

- Etc.

Silly? A stretch? Playing with words? Not really. This kind of hairsplitting results from trying to pin specific meanings to mushy words—words that mean different things to different people in different situations. Mush words are words that have a subjective rather than objective meaning. Neither *stop* nor *thief* are mush words; everyone who knows those words also knows what they mean in general use. On the other hand, while virtually everyone knows generally what *love* means, it *is* a mush word. If you ask nine people to define it, you are likely to come up with nine slightly different (and perhaps slightly incompatible) interpretations.

In his book, *Unlimited Power* (mentioned in Chapter Two), Anthony Robbins commented, "The way we communicate with others and with ourselves ultimately determines the quality of our lives."

This chapter—this book—is not about casual conversation where you may not be paying particular attention to what's going on:

- "Hi, how are you doing?"

- "Well, I totaled my car yesterday."

- "Glad to hear it. Take care, now."

Silly example? Well, lately I (Bob) have noticed when I enter a store, a salesperson will say "Hello," but when I say "Hello" back, they answer "Fine, thanks." Disconnected, are they? Telegraphing their lack of genuine interest, are they?

So the material in this chapter concerns theories, tips, and techniques to help you and your partner become more precise when speaking with one another. We are assuming these suggestions will be applied to conversations that are meant to be important, connected, and imbued with genuine interest.

Basic skills

Rules of engagement

You are part of a team and you are tackling an issue of some kind. Your purpose and your intent is to work with one or more people towards a win/win conclusion. Here are some points that may help you:

- **Create an emotional safe space.** Make an agreement that nothing said by one person will be weaponized and used against them.

- **Concentrate on one issue at a time.** Multitasking is not your friend. You can stop discussing a new point (and move on to the next topic) once you reach a satisfactory resolution of the original point.

- **Make sure everyone understands each statement before moving on to the next.** Use active listening practices combined with NVC (Nonviolent Communication) strategies.

- **Listen to understand one another.** Don't wait for your chance to defend your position or convince them you are right.

- **Work together to remove emotional reactions and listen in neutral.** Don't attach emotional value to what is being said.

- **Develop and use your *exit strategy* when you need a break.** This is simply a nonviolent way to end a heated discussion. An effective exit strategy includes an agreement to reengage later, once emotions cool off.

Problem-solving approaches

Perhaps the easiest way of changing your emotional state is to alter your physical position. If you are sitting, stand up. If you are standing, sit down or walk around. However, there is a caution here: If the person with whom you are speaking is emotionally upset or angry, suddenly changing your physical position may be interpreted as a threat (or insult, or a demonstration of your lack of care about the topic) and escalate the situation.

The more you know about yourself and your reactions under stress (and the more you know about your listener and *their* reactions under stress), the better. Greater knowledge in these areas will help you to manage emotionally-based discussions. At the very least, breathe slowly and deeply and keep control of your facial muscles.

When you encounter resistance within yourself or another, you are likely to want to reestablish stability in order to work through the situation. In such cases, consider breaking your current pattern of interaction. More formally, this is called a *state change* (*state* here means *emotional state*).

State change is really important if you have lost rapport with the other person. Perhaps one of you said or did something that was not taken well. You can ignore this incident and continue as though nothing happened. But then, one or both of you will be *stuffing* your emotional reactions. Or you can try to fix whatever came up. To repair the situation, you will want to know how to use state change to get back to rapport.

This leads directly to a method for applying knowledge during an upset. Let's say you and the person with whom you are speaking have had an upset. Something came up and one or both of you flared. The discussion became heated. Your feelings were hurt; their feelings were hurt. It's been a few days and you have both decided it's time to speak again. How exactly do you sit down to work through an emotionally charged discussion?

Our suggestions in the bullet points below were developed over time from books and from our own observations. Here is a list of the high-level components that underlie the communication strategy we are about to describe:

- In negotiations, people seated across from one another are more argumentative than people sitting next to one another.

- Physical contact builds or maintains rapport between people.

- Some challenges are internal (relationship issues) and some are external (something from the world is acting upon you).

- Virtually everyone in modern society is living with stress; it's just a matter of how much stress. When sitting down to work through a relationship issue, outside stress may make the discussion doubly difficult. Most stress in the U.S. centers around finances, health, family, and work.

- Seldom will two people have an identical understanding of an event, even if both of them were holding hands and watching it together. Everybody's worldview is unique, and their worldview affects their reactions to events.

- There are well-known techniques to help people understand the ways they frame (interpret) events and then shift that perspective to reframe (reinterpret) it positively. In a general sense, *dissonance resolution* describes the process of subconsciously reinterpreting an event in such a way that it now appears you were not at fault.

- While you cannot change external conditions, you can certainly change your response to those conditions.

Based on those premises, what we (ourselves) do and recommend you consider doing is this:

- **Sit side-by-side on a couch** (or in two chairs). Make sure neither of you feel as though there are boundaries between you, such as bulky armrests or too much space.

- **Orient your bodies so you are not squared off.** It's important to be looking in the same direction, perhaps into the room or at an object in front of you. Structuring sensitive discussions this way should help keep you from fight-or-flight mode. Remember that neither of you is the problem. The problem is out there. You are a team handling an issue.

- **Don't make a lot of *you* statements.** This isn't about blame or proving one of you is more right than the other.

- **Touch hands or each place a hand on the other's leg** (if appropriate). Touching someone can release oxytocin, which helps us to relax and feel good. This also will inhibit that fight-or-flight pattern. Obviously, you don't use this strategy with a co-worker.

- **Bring only the most important items to the table.** A litany of complaints confuses the immediate issue. The order of importance gets lost. Focus on one or two things. Work through them thoroughly.

- **Bring a notebook and pen (or computer) to the discussion.** Don't interrupt when the other person is speaking. You can make some notes about what to bring up later. This helps you stay present and in the moment. It removes your need to concentrate on remembering what you wish to say next and enables you to truly listen to understand.

Exit strategy

Each of us has experienced upsets. We have all been through the experience of rising emotions. Here's a tip: Develop a plan to de-escalate emotionally heated discussions. If your plan turns out to be unsuccessful, have a back-up plan (a communications *exit strategy*) to disengage, re-evaluate, and re-engage once everyone's emotions are under control. These are our suggestions:

- **Set a timer.** Limit the length of time allotted for the discussion. Don't feel you have to cram every assorted complaint into one negotiated discussion. Agree that another meeting can occur. Some people need time or distance to process thoughts and feelings; others prefer to remain in the conversation until issues are resolved. Those two types can drive each other batty. Consider setting a time limit for emotional discussions so both people can remain engaged yet feel safe in that space.

- **Agree on time-outs.** If someone needs a break, decide ahead of time what that looks like. How long can it be? What can both parties do during that time? Note: This is a well-defined break in the discussion, and everyone engaged has, presumably, agreed to see it through. No, you can't run into town and do some shopping.

- **Repeat what you think you heard.** Before moving on, wait for the other person to confirm that your understanding was correct.

- **Forget about needing to be right.** Would you rather be right or in a relationship (or have a job)? FYI, being right doesn't make you breakfast in the morning, but your partner might. Proving a point can sometimes be so important that we become insensitive about one another's emotions. Remember: Being right is irrelevant in the larger scheme of things.

- **Be prepared to make concessions.** In real estate, I (Veronica) tell my clients that it is usually a good deal when every party is slightly dissatisfied. That might not be a bad motto for resolving conflicts as well.

- **Your exit strategy isn't an escape.** It's a planned way to de-escalate the situation. You re-engage once calmer emotions give you a better chance of success. Engaging your exit strategy is not a failure. It is an opportunity to remove biases and filters to increase your chances of a successful outcome for all.

By the way, remember with whom you are speaking. This is a living, breathing human being, not an archvillain from your favorite action movie. This other person is not out to get you. They are struggling to communicate. They are trying to express their needs. They want to connect just as much as you do.

Speaking

As you've just read, we distinguish between *talking* and *speaking*. People *talk to* someone or *speak with* someone. *Talking to* someone is a one-way street. It's lecturing. By its very nature, the lecturer shares information in a controlled situation.

We strongly advise you not to *talk to* your partner at any time; it's demeaning and connotes that the other person has nothing valuable to share.

You can get into trouble *talking to* someone during an emotionally charged exchange because when you sound authoritative, you also sound *parental*. Those familiar with transactional analysis (TA, previously mentioned—and to be discussed in depth in Chapter Six) realize that speaking in *parent voice* can trigger (or sustain) your listener responding in *child voice* (filled with emotion-laden words). Talking in parent voice can also trigger defensiveness. Being talked down to creates resentment. Once you know a bit about TA, you'll learn how to extract yourself from this kind of loop by moving into what is called *adult voice*.

We assert that the path to effective adult conversation involves *speaking with* someone using clear and neutral words. Let's tease this apart for a minute. All communication involves the following mix:

• Someone wishes to communicate a message.

• They say something that may or may not communicate that message clearly.

- Even if the speaker actually succeeds in saying the words that carried their intended message, the listener receives the message within the context of personal, social, political, and economic filters created from their lifetime of experiences. We are all most strongly influenced by our childhood, around which we build life rules that keep us from emotional or physical pain.

- In an effort to make what was said fit into their universe, the listener interprets what they think they heard and makes it mean something. However, that something may not be precisely what the speaker intended to communicate. As Mark Twain said, "The difference between the right word and the almost right word is the difference between lightning and a lightning bug."

We have mentioned this once before, but it's important enough to repeat. Speaking is rather like sex. We think we do it well because we've been doing it all our lives. In reality, we seldom sit down to study either topic. Unfortunately, when we do something for which we have not been trained, we seldom do it very well. That's true for sex and it is also true for communication. Most people tend to experience mediocre sex and imprecise communication.

You might reflect for a minute:

- What evidence do you have that you are able to communicate clearly, confidently, and persuasively? In your work life, are you looked upon as a particularly clear communicator?

- Do your ideas have selling power? Do other people generally follow your ideas? (By the way, if you are in sales or marketing fields, the book *Words that Sell* by Richard Bayan may interest you.)

- Have you read books, taken courses, or attended conferences in effective communication strategies?

- When you speak, do you use simple words, short sentences, and clear word-pictures?

- When your partner describes an experience or a concern, do you take the time to listen actively and then respond in a way that makes them feel acknowledged and respected? Does the person with whom you are speaking feel valued and validated?

Listening

It upsets people when they feel they are not being heard. Whether at home or at work, this is one of the most common communication complaints. Fortunately, communication skills (like other skills) improve through practice. In our experience, even *realizing* there are different listening levels has helped both of us to focus and be mindful when listening to others. We pass these techniques on to you in the hopes you find them equally useful.

Listening begins with basic sound discrimination when you are first born. As we mentioned a few pages ago, a baby cries, stops, listens for a reaction, and continues crying. Your listening skills become refined as you develop into adulthood. Some adults have outstanding listening skills; others, not so much. If you would like to explore this topic, we recommend *Crucial Conversations* by Kerry Patterson, et al. (previously mentioned in Chapter Two).

While listening takes many forms, this list of eight common listening styles are enough to give you an overview:

1 **Discriminative listening.** This is the most basic type of receptive communication. This is where you learn how to assign meaning to sounds and to interpret voice inflections and emotional nuances. During a conversation, the richness of your

understanding depends upon your skills at recognizing and interpreting the speaker's emotional cues.

Discriminative listening is closely allied to discriminative *observation*. It means that when listening, you're trying to pick up shades of meaning. You are trying to interpret the speaker based on what you know about the person. As a resource, we highly recommend a book mentioned in the last chapter: *What Every BODY is Saying* by Joe Navarro and Marvin Karlins.

2   **Comprehension listening.** This simply means that you're combining your vocabulary, language, and social skills to understand both the speaker's words and their intended meaning. Even when English is your native language, complications can jump uninvited into conversations. Comprehension listening becomes important under three common conditions:

1   The speaker uses imprecise words, leaving meanings open to interpretation.

2   The speaker uses filler words (e.g. *stuff*, *things*) forcing you to guess what they are talking about.

3   The speaker is using coded or indirect speech meant to be understood only by certain people, and that might not include you.

3   **Critical listening.** This enables you to evaluate and judge what is said—as long as the speaker is using clear and direct speech. Critical listening requires more than simply understanding what is being said. This form of listening includes the ability to relate what is said to what you know about that topic while simultaneously reading the person's nonverbal cues.

Critical listening skills have to be developed. As Peter Drucker said in an interview with Bill Moyers on one episode of the

1989 television show, *A World of Ideas*: "The most important thing in communication is hearing what isn't said." To do this, you have to stay present and focused on the speaker.

So, for example, you'll want to overcome the normal tendency to become distracted by self-talk filled with judgments and considerations. You'll want to stay focused even if the speaker misuses a word or says something that you believe is not true. Similarly, you have to avoid becoming distracted from the core conversation by looking for subtext. Some people do not clearly say what they mean; they use a kind of code or subtext to disguise uncomfortable topics. As a listener, you risk becoming distracted trying to decipher subtext while simultaneously staying present with the ongoing conversation. That's a form of *multitasking*. Ample current research clearly shows that multitasking confuses your brain, as you have to switch between two (or more) topics. Your slowed brain expresses its unhappiness by reducing overall performance.

4   **Biased listening.** This can occur for many reasons. Commonly, the speaker says something that annoys (or triggers) you; your listening is compromised. Your brain reacts by shifting focus from the speaker to yourself. You are going to concentrate mainly on what *you* deem relevant. As the speaker continues, you'll miss parts of the message.

At this stage, your own stereotypes, insecurities, and assumptions about the speaker or the topic may cause you to further misinterpret what is being said. In emotional conversations, it is *very common* for a speaker to say one thing and for the listener to hear something wildly different. Of course, the listener can only react to what they think they heard, often adding to the upset. In business settings (and even in some personal contexts), the leader is responsible for recognizing when this happens and to track down the root of the misunderstanding. It is important to take that step if you expect to prevent the same type of misinterpretation in the future. You do this by checking in with your listener to confirm they understand what you are saying.

5   **Appreciative listening.** This occurs when you are in a good mood and listening to something you enjoy. This could be music, poetry, or maybe just what the speaker is saying. Often, appreciative listening evokes feelings of gratitude; that's a good thing.

6   **Sympathetic listening.** This is used when we care about the other person and show this concern by paying close attention and expressing sorrow for their ills and happiness for their joys. (By the way, *empathetic* listening requires us to go beyond sympathy to seek a more complete picture of how others are feeling. This requires thoughtful discrimination and close attention to nuanced emotional signals. When we are being empathetic, we often experience what the speaker is feeling.)

7   **Relationship listening.** This is most common when the bond is new, and each verbal exchange adds to your pool of knowledge about your partner. This form of listening also occurs when there is an upset, and you are trying to understand the other person's viewpoint.

8   **Therapeutic listening.** This can be risky if you are not a trained therapist. With some trepidation, we are going to include it here. Psychologists and trained counselors use therapeutic listening to help clients understand, change, or develop in some way. That is, a client brings a problem to the therapist who listens with a *therapeutic ear* and replies in specific ways that encourage the client to explore their issue. Since the therapist is endeavoring to guide the patient, this style of listening can create an imbalance that is not good for personal relationships. Your listener may take your tone as condescending.

We have been discussing some of the fundamental aspects of speaking and listening. Now, we are going to move on to suggest ways to help improve communication skills.

Being engaging

There are ways to engage in an important discussion, and there are ways *not* to engage in an important discussion. This section offers some ideas to help you improve communication in everyday life. We are going to cover four topics in this section:

1   The intent of your questions

2   The clarity of your speech

3   Reacting

4   Active listening

The intent of your questions

It's not only *what* you say; it's *how* you say it. You know that.

> All true questions are neutral. If a question is not neutral, then it is not really a question, but rather a statement, or a judgment, disguised as a question. . . . Neutral questions increase intimacy, whereas non-neutral questions create defensiveness and distance.
>
> It is not enough for the words to be neutral. The intent of the questioner must also be neutral.

So wrote Charles MacInerney in his article, "The Importance of Neutral Questions."

For example, let's say that a co-worker is going on break. You say, "When are you going to be back from the fifth break you've had today?" Your colleague reacts strongly. They become defensive. They may say something nasty, they may feel shamed, they shut down emotionally. They may not even go on break. What the speaker doesn't know is that their co-worker has a health issue that causes them to frequently visit the restroom. The speaker may genuinely want to know when their co-worker is coming back because there is a meeting in a few minutes. However, the employee is now focused on being judged for how often they are taking breaks.

The message: Stay neutral when crafting your phrasing. Avoid expressing anger or judgment. Ask only the question that will gain you the information you require. For example, "Can you be back in about 15 minutes? We're having a team meeting."

A question should refrain from exposing your own judgments, biases, and personal filters. Neutral questions open the space for the other person to think about what was asked and respond appropriately.

We tend to make judgments about others in our lives. We have learned our own lessons and (foolishly) made the usual error that other people think (or problem-solve) as we do. We have already mentioned *the usual error*. It is an important concept, as it tends to be our default mindset, and it keeps tripping us up. In the case of neutral questions, this bias causes us to make judgments about others based upon insufficient evidence that we have drawn from *our* perspective. The error: *Instead of putting ourselves in their shoes, we put them in our shoes.*

A loaded question, frequently phrased sarcastically, contains our own judgments. Often these judgments are wrong and hurt our relationships with others.

Again, MacInerney:

> Neutral questions present an opportunity to clarify a situation prior to forming an opinion. Other times neutral questions arise from a belief that the other person may well have something more that they can share. Neutral questions should never be used as a back handed way to point out a perceived mistake or deficiency.

Here are some advantages to using neutral questions:

- **They help slow you down.** They help you become present with the situation and think more deeply before asking a question. (As Jim Hayhurst, Sr. said in his book, *The Right Mountain: Lessons from Everest on the Real Meaning of Success*, "When you don't know what to do, do it slowly.")

- **They are open-ended.** They are intended to encourage you to make a thoughtful reply. Thoughtful replies are good; they lead you down the path to meaningful communication.

- **They avoid revealing a personal agenda.** They communicate your open heart and open mind.

- **They enable you to explain your beliefs or actions without inviting any pre-drawn suspicions or conclusions.** This can provide mutually valuable information, for it enables you and the person you are communicating with to explore differences or similarities in your beliefs and assumptions about a topic.

That being said, there are levels of neutrality.

Questions that at first seem unbiased can mask buried agendas, biases, or opinions. It takes practice to develop the skill of asking truly impartial questions. Nevertheless, it's worth the effort (in our opinion). Biased questions lead to biased answers that may, in fact, be hiding the truth you are seeking.

Neutral questions lead us towards understanding. When a problem is transparent, the solution is easier to see.

The clarity of your speech

We all speak. For the most part, we think we are understood. The thing of it is, we all speak well enough for the level of interaction we're used to. We are not very sensitive to how much more clearly we *could* speak if we paid greater attention to our own words. Since we are largely unaware of how we speak, we are also not very aware of how clear and lucid speech would affect our lives. After all, first impressions are not only comprised of how we dress, stand, and walk. Such things as cultural expectations, accent/dialect, vocabulary, and clarity (to name a few) strongly influence the initial impressions we give others.

When speaking informally, particularly with friends, we tend to use imprecise words because the general meaning is obvious. Anyway, our friends sort of know what we mean. Thus, a sentence like this one: *I have to run. I've got to pick up some stuff before going home* makes perfect sense in an informal setting. Nobody is expecting you to actually run at that moment; nobody is interested in what you have to pick up before getting home.

The sophistication of the conversation affects the quality of your speech. You are more precise with your speech when necessary.

You can use baby talk with infants; you can't use baby talk with your boss. You may use a fairly informal level of speech with your boss, but not if your board chair is included in the conversation.

Speech quality should match the situation when conversations become more socially, politically, or professionally important. At least, that's how it is theoretically. Here are some areas to consider if you wish to increase your communication skills:

- Avoid filler words (*uh, um, stuff, things*, etc.)

- Increase your vocabulary (the larger your vocabulary and the more meanings you understand for words, the easier it is to communicate concepts)

- Eschew slang and idioms (keep it clear and concise)

- Enunciate clearly (don't mumble)

- Note your pace, tone, and pitch (go for slow and low)

- Pre-plan your sentences (pause before responding)

- Pay attention to your breathing (shallow breathing communicates nervousness and anxiety)

Words express concepts. Your sentences paint pictures. Try to rid yourself of mush words. They are like muddy colors.

"Oh, he brought some stuff over to my house; he wanted me to see his newest toy," gives no information beyond the fact that a man brought something unknowable to your abode. There is nothing in that sentence that encourages the listener to react. "Oh, Jack brought his new seven-inch Digibig Tablet over to my house last night. It was amazing; it weighed less than a pound. He was really excited to show me the new time-management apps that he's using. I think I'm going to go out and buy one!" Now we have solid information.

"I've never been so sad in all my life. I can't believe you did this to me," imparts no information beyond the fact that something is going on between you and the person with whom you are speaking, and that something is causing you to interpret their actions with emotional sadness. There is nothing here for you (or them) to empathize with or use to create a solution. "When you come home at night and sit for hours in front of the television without speaking, I take that to mean that you would rather not be here with me." Ah, solid information.

The sentence construction we used in that last paragraph follows a specific pattern meant to open yourself to the other person, so they understand the impact their words had on you. This gives them a chance to clarify what they said or to agree with the way you interpreted what they said. That is a *very* valuable tool. This is the pattern we mentioned about 30 pages ago: *When you said (or did) X, I made that mean Y.*

When you use the *I made that mean* sentence structure, you are explaining how you interpreted their actions or words.

This is extremely important when two people are trying to work through any kind of real or perceived emotional hurt. It also puts responsibility squarely back on the shoulders of the person feeling the emotion and perceiving the action.

An alternative to the *I made that mean* structure is simply to ask the person speaking to clarify what they just said. Ask, "What did you intend when you said...?" and repeat their statement. While this slows the conversation for a moment, it forces both of you to be present and deal with something that has the potential to be misunderstood. Taking the time to ask for clarification provides time for an emotional charge to dissipate.

This brings us to the next topic.

Reacting

When one person sees another person react to something they just said, the way the initial speaker reacts to that reaction depends on any number of things:

- The power or authority difference between the two people

- The communication and counseling skills of the speaker

- The speaker's interest in dealing with the other person's reaction

Apart from those large-scale topics, there are three communication setups that can lead to difficulties:

1   **The topic is one-sided.** Only one of you cares about the subject of the discussion. The other person isn't listening carefully and may miss most or all of the message.

2   **The message triggers something else.** On the positive side, the speaker may have triggered memories and the listener has gone off (into their head) to enjoy them. On the negative side, what the speaker said may have hit a hot button or a landmine, and the listener's feelings have been hurt (or the listener has become angry, etc.).

3   **The message sounds like a lecture.** The speaker *talks at* (lectures) the other person in a way that does not welcome responses. The listener feels like they are being talked down to (diminished, disrespected); they stop listening or build negative feelings about the speaker.

There are significant risks when one person becomes reactive and stops listening. The ignored speaker may become angry (or hurt or embarrassed) when they realize that the listener didn't seem to understand or retain the intended message and didn't probe for more information or a deeper understanding.

When situations such as these continue, one person may begin emotionally shutting down to protect their own feelings. They may begin to withdraw. In a general way, they are reacting to their perception of what they thought they heard.

LISTENING AND RESPONDING IN NEUTRAL

We recently discussed the importance of asking neutral questions. There is a technique that can help you avoid having (or expressing) reactions to things others say to you. The idea is to remain neutral as the listener. The trick to remaining neutral in your responses is to *become aware of what you are about to say before you say it.*

Whenever possible, try to avoid automatically agreeing or disagreeing with people. We know this sounds radical. However, this mindful practice will train you to control your beliefs and make you aware of your own viewpoints. You'll gain flexibility and control over your words.

Finally, using active listening techniques will help you to avoid prematurely agreeing or disagreeing with someone. Active listening (discussed in the next section) is repeating what another person said and not moving forward in the conversation until the speaker agrees you have heard them correctly.

Oh, and watch your body language. Frequently, we agree or disagree with an unintended nod or shake of our head. Other times, we may signal our discord by crossing our arms or legs or turning our body toward or away from the person speaking. A facial expression can send a message as powerful as hurtful words.

Listening and responding in neutral is especially important when someone wants you to agree with them or is trying to get you to disagree with them so they can defend their position. Listening neutrally disarms the speaker. In conversations, we generally expect supportive feedback. Getting a different (new) response increases the odds of better, more sincere understanding.

It takes conscious practice to develop this skill. Neutral listening is an act of mindfulness not taught in our culture. We are used to automatically replying to people. This new skill requires us to pay close attention to our own replies during normal conversations. It can be a challenge to become an observer of our own words. Observing our own words leads to observing our own thoughts.

As Gary van Warmerdam says in his outstanding *Self Mastery* courses (which can be found at <u>pathwaytohappiness.com</u>), "By keeping your responses neutral, you will avoid giving away your own personal power to their position or point of view. You are building your personal power by not wasting it." (We also highly recommend his book *MindWorks: A Practical Guide for Changing Thoughts, Beliefs and Emotional Reactions.*)

Van Warmerdam (whose material has strongly influenced this section of the book and is included here with his permission) points out that people waste their personal power (and burn up their emotional capital) when they judge the world around them with snide or negative thoughts. Examples include: *Wow, what a stupid driver, I hate my job*, or *Well, she certainly has no fashion sense!*

When someone makes a statement to you, you can conserve your personal power by staying in neutral and replying:

- "I won't disagree with you."

- "I hear you."

- "That's an interesting perspective!"

When you are asked questions meant to evoke *yes* answers, you can reply:

- "Well, I don't have a firm opinion about that."

- "That's interesting."

- "Well, I need to give that more thought."

Part of the art of neutral replies is to be so smooth that your lack of agreement isn't obvious; you do not want to appear evasive.

You'll also want to avoid stating (or agreeing with) something that is phrased as a universal truth. For example, "This constant rain makes everyone depressed, doesn't it?" is phrased as a universal statement prompting another person to agree or disagree. Your reply (if you are a rain lover) does not have to be polarizing. You can just state the neutral fact, "It definitely is raining."

It is a mindful practice to remain neutral in social interactions. However, it is not mindful to do this at work (for example) where you are being paid to give an opinion. You *can* begin your sentences with some version of: *From my perspective...* Soft openings invite others to bring up points you might not have considered. However, the power and impact of your words is reduced when you use qualifiers. You'll have to gauge how strongly you want your statements to be perceived.

Here is a subtle but important note: In all cultures we have a social agreement to get along with others. If you're *not* agreeing with someone, they might notice it. It will affect how they feel about you and also the stories they make up (and believe) about you. So, practice being smooth and invisible with it.

Active listening

If you care about understanding the person with whom you are speaking, you have to put some work into the conversation. You must stay present. Conversations have four elements:

1   The words themselves

2   The subtext (hidden meanings) behind the words (that may be discovered by realizing what the speaker is *not* including in the conversation)

3   Non-verbal cues (gestures and mannerisms)

4   Emotions and tone

You can usually tell when someone has checked out of a conversation. They aren't responding appropriately (or at all). They are *drifting.* Their body is starting to face away from you, they aren't making eye contact, etc. Either they have grabbed onto something you said and are following that trail, or they are thinking about something else that has distracted them from the conversation. Either way, their lack of interest shows.

There are some easy and tactful ways of pulling yourself or a drifting partner back into the conversation:

• **If you're having trouble staying present.** "Excuse me for a minute, let me get a glass of water; I'll be right back."

• **If you want to be more open and honest.** "Sorry, I let my attention drift, what was that again?"

- **If you sense the listener is not paying attention.** "Perhaps we can discuss this at another time. Let's stop this conversation for now and pick it up later."

- **If you want to engage the listener.** "You seem to be pondering something. What is it?"

If you want to go one step further, consider one of our favorite communication tools: *active listening*. Active listening comes up again section after next, we'll introduce the technique to you at this point.

It can be a challenge to remember to use active listening, but both of us are impressed when someone uses this technique. Veronica and I particularly appreciate this tool because it has the added advantage of expressing respect for the person with whom you are speaking. Active listening demonstrates that you are paying attention.

Active listening is the bridge between speaking and listening. This is true for both parties. Active listening demonstrates that the conversation (and the person with whom you are speaking) has value. Many people find active listening to be a challenge. They can only do it for only a few minutes before they just have to voice their own opinion. Practicing neutral responses for a while will help you conserve your personal power and break the habit of unconsciously jumping in with your opinion. This will set you up for more success as an active listener.

Here's how it works. When Person A says something, Person B restates what Person A said rather than responding immediately to the topic. Person A can now correct or refine Person B's interpretation of what they had initially said. Once everyone has a clear and cohesive understanding, Person B can correctly respond. This response is interpreted and restated by Person A. Rinse and repeat as necessary.

Speaking this way provides three immediate benefits:

1   It improves the quality of the conversation by slowing the conversation to give each person time to think, digest, understand, and responsibly reply.

2   It improves clarity which is easily muddled during rapid exchanges. The listener has time to realize they may have misheard or misinterpreted something.

3   It removes emotional loading from conversations. Everyone can remain calm.

Here is a well-known example. If someone were to say "The fish are ready to eat," a person using active listening might ask "Let me make sure I understand you. Do you mean it is time to feed the fish?" Now, the somewhat surprised speaker might reply, "No, I mean that we are having fish for dinner tonight and they are cooked and ready to eat."

See: No chance for miscues. This type of communication is referred to as *adult-to-adult*, in the language of TA (transactional analysis), discussed in more depth in the next chapter.

Respectful processes such as these support relationships of all kinds. We have found active listening to be *extremely* helpful, particularly in potentially stressful discussions. You usually hear this technique used in mediation where a communication slip can have unfortunate consequences.

QUANTIFYING IMPORTANCE

There is one last technique to describe before we leave the topic of active listening. Everyone reading this book has experienced it. You ask your partner, "Where do you want to go for dinner?" They reply, "I don't care, where do you want to go?" This goes around and around for a while. This can be very frustrating. But there is a technique to reaching a painless decision. Ask, "On a 1–10 scale, how much would enjoy eating at x? Okay, on that same 1–10 scale, how about eating at y?"

This method of quantifying someone's reactions resolves quite a bit of communication frustration. You can use this technique on major or minor issues. "On a 1–10 scale, how much do you want to sell this house?" or "On a 1–10 scale, how interested are you in accepting this job offer?"

You must be clear that there is no punishment for honesty. Your purpose is to help one another reach a balanced decision. You're managing expectations by quantifying each other's needs. This is a fact-finding mission. You're just collecting information so you both have the most enjoyable experience possible.

WAYS OF PHRASING THINGS

In a general sense, we are all here on earth just trying to do the best we can and help others along the way. Our communication styles can make it easier or harder on ourselves and those around us. The way we phrase sentences helps or hinders the message. Here are some examples of gentle ways to respond to others:

- Asking for more information or verifying your understanding of something:

    - "Just to be sure I understand, you would like me to...?"

    - "Tell me more about..."

    - "So, you are saying that... correct?"

- "This is what I understand you are telling me..."

- Taking responsibility for answering a question if you don't know the answer:

  - "That's a good question. I don't have an immediate answer. Let me find out for you. You're asking... is that correct?"

  - "I apologize, I don't have information about that. If you'll hold the line, I'll check with my supervisor."

  - "I apologize. This issue is beyond my expertise. I don't believe I can help you, and I don't know enough about that topic to suggest any resources!"

- How to say *no* without triggering an upset:

  Saying no to someone can be off-putting to them. Depending upon the situation, it may be taken as confrontational and rude. The well-known *compliment sandwich* softens the message. John Rydell describes some effective alternatives in his article "Simple Tips on Having the Hard Conversation". Basically, he suggests recognizing the request up front, then adding positive statements that offer a viable compromise to your refusal.

  - "You want to have a weekend trip to Las Vegas. I get that. I would love to have a weekend with you where we can focus on each other. However, we cannot afford a long-distance trip right now. Although it's not Vegas, how about a romantic weekend getaway at a hotel here in town?"

  - "I understand that you would like a two-seater sports car. That sounds both zippy and fun. However, I think we would have trouble with a small car, considering our four children. How about four-wheel drive SUV that has a sporty feel? You can choose the color, interior, and upgrades!"

Making distinctions

Business executives are paid to make decisions. Often those decisions are based on incomplete information. Successful managers have learned to listen carefully and to ask questions that help them recognize the information they need to make good choices. However, this path contains some landmines. We are going to tackle two of them in this section: *the stated issue vs. the real issue* and *relationship expediency vs. tough alternatives.*

The stated issue vs. the real issue

Usually when people say they want to work on issue x (cleaning their closet, perhaps) the issue is x. That's a relatively simple, practical problem. However, sometimes x (cleaning their closet) isn't the real issue. It is only a symptom or an aspect of something much deeper, such as their overall lack of tidiness. You can learn more about the person with whom you're speaking when you sense (or realize) that the other person's expressed issue isn't the core problem. For example:

- The issue the person proposes to work on (cleaning their closet) may be a more approachable topic than the core concern (overall lack of tidiness).

- The issue the person wishes to discuss (cleaning their closet) may be a feint—a substitute issue that represents an emotionally safe alternative (perhaps they are afraid they are a hoarder). In fact, the other person may be hiding the real issue from you or from themselves.

- The person doesn't have the personal insight to realize the topic they've proposed (cleaning their closet) won't resolve their concern or upset.

- Your own blinders and filters cause you to incorrectly assess the importance of the topic the person wishes to discuss.

- You assume you understand what the person wants because if you were in their place, you would simply work on tidying your closet. You wouldn't have any anxiety about your own level of cleanliness or fears you might be a hoarder.

Sometimes people mean something quite specific when they speak— it's just that they are using their own special code. You can begin to suspect this has happened when you've worked through an issue, but your proposed solution seems unsatisfactory. When this happens, you might consider going back to your partner to explore what you heard them say. By the way, they may think they were very clear with you. They are so used to their own code, they won't understand how you could possibly misunderstand.

Sometimes what you *think* is the problem simply isn't the problem.

Here is a common situation. You've been partners for over ten years. One person identifies an issue they would like to discuss. This issue is easy for both of you to speak about because it isn't complicated. For example, one partner misses being kissed when the other partner returns home from work. Not a biggie; the returning partner realizes they have simply grown accustomed to having the other person around. That at-home person might feel silly to want to be kissed when the person they've lived with for over ten years comes home from work. But there it is.

As you begin discussing the topic, you realize how you greet one another upon arriving home from work is only a superficial aspect of a much larger question. The larger issue concerns how each of you expresses love for the other. You realize that changing this superficial behavior (greeting one another after work) fails to address the larger issue (lack of emotional connectedness) that triggered this discussion about kissing. Three divergent pathways come to mind:

4   **Avoid the core issue.** You resolve to kiss one another when you reconnect after work. You leave it at that. You either don't recognize the underlying issue or the underlying issue is simply too complicated to approach.

5   **Complete avoidance.** You back away from developing solutions even to an issue as small as the after-work kiss out of fear that other (spinoff) topics could get away from you—topics you're not prepared to discuss.

6   **Full engagement.** As you start down the emotional connectedness track, you realize that each of you are describing different behaviors that would make you feel more connected. That, in turn, starts a discussion about what it even means to be emotionally connected. That discussion in turn takes us to *How do we prefer to spend time together?* and that also reveals differences that are (in fact) opportunities for furthering a mutual sense of intimacy.

Now, rather than a simple lighthearted discussion about how you greet one another when coming home from work, you have some very raw, core value differences sitting on the table staring at you. Obviously, you realize that a simple welcome home ceremony won't solve the larger challenge.

This brings up a related topic that Professor Patrick Faircloth of Troy University brought up with us: the importance of building a common lexicon.

When I (Veronica) begin a new relationship, I begin by building a common vocabulary. I do this by unpacking what certain key words mean for each of us. This is a very important step for me. I need to be sure that we have common definitions for key words (such as *love, upset, mad, happy, relationship, fine,* etc.).

You skip this step at your own peril.

For example, I had a partner (a native New Yorker) who, when we disagreed, claimed I was screaming at him. I was shocked and immediately became defensive. In my world, screaming is very, very, very unladylike and offensive. Screaming, in my world, demonstrates a lack of personal self-control.

This was only his perception, of course. I do not raise my voice when I'm upset. I become quieter and my voice drops an octave.

We would lose sight of the point of contention as we both reacted to our individual definitions of the words *scream* and *yell*. As we unpacked his definition of screaming, we found that in his family of origin, the person who was the loudest and carried on the longest won most arguments. Even though I don't raise my voice, the simple act of having an opposing opinion was connected in his emotional self to screaming. When he would say that I was screaming, I became mortified that he would even *think* I was raising my voice.

Once I gained control over my response to his words, he was able to be less defensive during disagreements. We added a new (common) definition of what *yelling* or *screaming* meant into our relationship lexicon. Then we were able to (once again) re-engage about actual issues as opposed to being thrown off by the conflicting emotional charge those words had for each of us.

So... when your discussions (with anyone) reveal some degree of conflict or possible misunderstanding, the first step toward a solution is to explore (unpack) what the key words mean for each person and come up with a common lexicon.

Here is a great starter exercise for people in a relationship: Write the answer the question *What do each of you believe your relationship encompasses?* Try it out. Have the discussion. Each person writes down the components, hopes, and expectations of having a partner in a relationship. Everyone writes out their core relationship rules. Have you shared those with your partner(s)? This exercise can provide helpful insights into how you are viewed by others close to you.

At a deeper level, I (Bob) vividly recall the night one of my partners and I had our first "word understandings" discussion. It was triggered by her comment that she wanted me to be more transparent. I asked her what transparency meant to her, and how I would behave if I were more transparent. She easily described behaviors that (to her) meant I'd be transparent. Wow! New information.

However, since I am not neurotypical, I realized that she was asking for behaviors my brain wiring would fight.

As a person with high-functioning autism, I live in a compartmentalized world. I have multiple mini-lives going on at the same time. I have relationships with other people, and I am generally disinclined to share much about them. From my viewpoint, when I was with her, I was with her. The others belonged in their own compartments.

I explained that to her. She was not happy. She wanted to know all about everything I was doing in my life so she could share in my excitements and support my challenges. While I appreciated the sentiment, this was not who I am. I wasn't interested, and I wasn't sure I could even do it. I told her so. This became a sticking point that lasted as long as we were together.

Moral: You may discover values that don't mesh well once you start clarifying important word meanings.

If you haven't recently read *Men Are from Mars, Women Are from Venus* by John Gray, we urge you to revisit it. Gray discusses gender differences and socialization, and how these play out in conversations and relationships.

Relationship expediency vs. tough alternatives

There is a common misconception that you shouldn't have to work at a relationship; if it's meant to be, it's going to go smoothly. Others (including us) hold the view that if you aren't *working* on your relationship, you really aren't *in* a relationship.

When someone in a relationship chooses an easy path, they may be choosing simplicity and speed over solid resolution. They may be choosing quick vs. permanent; quick vs. a lasting and stable solution. This may happen when the two or more of you discover a point of friction that is going to take real work to resolve. You both realize that by ignoring this particular issue, you are purposefully substituting a quick-and-dirty solution to avoid making a tough decision. You've chosen a Band-Aid over surgery.

In that light, this book has been about communication issues. Specifically, it's been about *resolvable* communication issues. Not all communication issues are resolvable. Some communication issues have to do with brain wiring. People think differently. Furthermore, people have different verbal IQ capabilities. This book is *not* about solving serious or deep-seated challenges that are manifesting through communication problems. In those cases, communication itself may not be the issue. Seeking professional help is worth checking out.

Mitigated speech

David O'Hare first used the term *mitigated speech* in his book, *Flightdeck Performance: The Human Factor*. The word was further popularized by Malcolm Gladwell in his book, *Outliers*. He defined mitigated speech as *any attempt to downplay or sugarcoat the meaning of what is being said*.

O'Hare created this phrase by analyzing pilot and copilot conversations that had been recovered from flight recorders after airline crashes. He made two very interesting discoveries. First, most crashes occurred when the pilot was in command, not when the copilot was flying the plane. Second, there was a correlation between airline crashes and the cultures in which the copilots were raised. In brief, to the extent that copilots came from cultures with high regard for people with authority, they were less likely to speak directly about a problem. They found ways of sugarcoating bad news.

Ultimately, psychologists identified six degrees of mitigation we use when speaking with supervisory staff who have authority over us. We have found these distinctions to be illuminating when it comes to nuanced conversations. This progressive ladder of phrasing enables the speaker to "slice the apple" a number of ways to indicate increased concern over an issue:

1   Hint. "Could run into any roadblocks on our current course?"

2   Preference. "Let's take a look at one of these Y alternatives."

3   Query. "Do you think strategy X would help us in this situation?"

4   Suggestion. "Why don't we try strategy X?"

5   Obligation. "We need to try strategy X."

6   Command. "Strategy X is going to be implemented."

The way the airline industry has sought to resolve the (often fatal) perils of mitigated speech apply directly to this book on interpersonal communication.

Whether flying an airplane or being in a committed relationship, some of us wither and withdraw when someone confronts us, even though we suspect they are not factually correct.

For the airline industry, this problem of pilot/copilot communication is divided into two parts: first, getting the copilot to view the pilot as a person like themself (rather than someone with authority over them); and second, creating specific words or phrases the copilot can use to communicate truly serious problems to the pilot.

The first step calls for the copilot to *use the pilot's first name* with the following speech protocols. The use of the pilot's first name (as opposed to calling them *captain*, per standard protocols) is the first signal that the message that follows is very important for the pilot to understand. So, let's say that the pilot's name is André. The three phrases available to the copilot are these:

- "André, I'm concerned about..."

- "André, I'm uncomfortable with..."

- "André, I believe the situation is unsafe."

If the pilot has not responded to correct the problem and the copilot continues to believe the aircraft is in immediate peril, they then have the authority to take command of the aircraft.

If you are used to living and working in an egalitarian setting, there can be some challenges translating this system to a work or home situations. After all, you are probably used to calling your supervisor, workmates, and domestic partner by their first names. Some readers may be able to signal an important message by speaking more formally. For example:

- Use Mr., Ms., Mrs., or Dr. either with their first name ("Mr. Bob, I'm concerned about...") or with their last name ("Mr. Rubel, I'm concerned about...").

- If you're used to using a pet name or nickname for your partner, you can revert to their legal name ("Robert, I'm concerned about...").

- You are also likely to get their attention by including their first and middle names or their entire names ("Robert Jack, I'm concerned about..." or "Robert Rubel, I'm concerned about...").

You knew how upset your parents were with you by the number of your names they strung together when scolding you over some incident. If all three (or more) of your names were used (first–middle–last), you knew you were in serious trouble!

Clearly, you'll have to discuss this safety alert system and work out a signal that will work for you. You'll also have to practice it a time or two in order to connect the idea that an unusual way of addressing your partner is part of a signaling system that something is going wrong and requires their focused, immediate attention.

Consider the possibility that some of your communication challenges have resulted from your desire to respect authority. Most of us are taught to respect authority, and such respect has its place. However, showing respect doesn't mean you are to permit someone you feel has more authority than you (or more experience or seniority) to misinterpret you or make a mistake that would affect an important outcome.

Now that you know about mitigated speech, you have specialized knowledge. There is no advantage in having specialized knowledge or skills unless you use them. This system of overcoming mitigated speech enables you to alert your partner to your level of concern about the relationship itself or about some aspect of your relationship. You can also use these codes when you are in public and need to signal an upset to your partner without making a scene.

Talking sticks

Talking sticks are a nonviolent method of settling disagreements first developed by Native Americans.

I (Bob) like talking sticks. I like the idea of using a physical action to break up an emotional upset. I have used them to work through everything from large problems to recurring upsets.

In a personal setting, anyone may request a session. Talking sticks are intended to slow the conversation. This slowing down has the effect of removing emotion from the exchange and forcing each person to confirm that what the other person said was accurate.

Here is the process:

- The two (or more) of you sit down facing one another.

- The talking stick (anything you can pick up and hold) is in the middle, perhaps on something ceremonial (a piece of leather, a silk scarf).

- The person who asked for the meeting picks up the stick and gives a one-sentence summary of the issue. It is very important to limit the conversation to a single idea.

- The talking stick is then placed back down between the speakers.

- The stick is then picked up by the second person, so long as they remain *willing* to participate in this process. This second person now repeats what they heard the first person say and then puts the stick down.

- The first person again picks up the stick and either agrees that the second person correctly understood what they said, or the first person corrects the second person's version of what they said.

- The first person then puts the stick down. This process goes on as long as necessary until the first person agrees that the second person understood the opening statement.

- Once both people know what the first person meant, the second person may frame a one-sentence response.

- The stick is again placed between them and is picked up by the first person.

- You are now in a repeating pattern. The first person repeats (paraphrases) the second person's reply to the initial statement. The second person confirms or rejects the first person's reply. By using the talking stick, both parties will eventually understand the nature of the upset and create a path out of the difficulty.

Someone I know who uses this system explained that over the years it only became necessary to use talking sticks when the situation is so emotionally charged that those involved have raised their defenses.

Venting

A woman who is having intense emotions about an issue may want to describe the situation (and her feelings about it) without getting advice or problem-solving suggestions in return. She just wants to feel heard. This helps her to recover her equilibrium. By the way, men may not like to admit it, but they frequently need to vent as well.

Home after work (or out to lunch with friends), a woman has a friendly ear. She wants someone to share the injustice of it all. Men, who tend to be solution-oriented, often want to be helpful and are inclined to offer suggestions.

You may want to hold that thought. A misstep here is likely to draw you into bad drama. You might want to consider a line of approach that asks, "Would you like me to help solve this with you, or would you prefer that I listen to you with a sympathetic ear?"

If they ask for your input, input away.

However, if you don't have specific permission to inject your good ideas, permit us to offer you a set of *okay responses*:

- "Wow!"

- "I could see how that would upset you."

- "People can certainly surprise you, can't they?"

- "It baffles me how someone could do that."

- "I see."

- "You handled that very well."

- And so forth.

Often, people who are venting wish to relate an experience just to get it out of their systems. The very *last* thing they want is for some-one to tell them what they *should have done* or what they *should do tomorrow* to fix it. They may not be interested in hearing your ideas about solving it. They are plenty smart, and they understand their work politics much better than you do. If *they* don't know how to fix it, it's unlikely you do, either. Anyway, they may not want it fixed. Or it may be a situation that has to be endured. Some things are better left alone.

Unless you are pretty sophisticated at listening for word prompts that signal emotional states, you risk replying in *parent voice* (making authoritative pronouncements and offering solutions) rather than replying in *adult voice* (that is neutral and free of emotions). Replying with *coulds* and *shoulds* (in an authoritative, parent voice) will likely trigger a negative emotional reaction which will only exacerbate the bad feelings that triggered the venting in the first place.

That last paragraph is the technical way of saying that if you are not careful, you will make matters much worse. Speaking in parent voice during a venting session may well cause the person with whom you're speaking to drop into *child voice* (filled with emotional statements). Once that happens, the conversation is likely to refocus on what an ass you are.

Our advice: Beware, you might hit an emotional landmine. If you're curious about ways that word choice can help or hurt your more serious relationship discussions, you can look up transactional analysis. We describe TA in Chapter Six in the section titled "Ego States."

Improper listening is as damaging as improper speaking. They are equal sides of the communication equation. What can you do? You can become a better listener.

How can I practice good listening habits? you ask. Here are some of our suggestions.

Give full attention

You can use someone's venting time as a practice session for your listening skills. When someone is venting, they want to be heard. They trust you or they wouldn't be venting to you. The most helpful thing you can do is shut up and pay attention.

Paying attention is a good habit for listening (particularly when someone is venting). Attentive listening involves more than your ears, it involves your whole body. Turn to face them. Make eye contact. Read their body language. *Attentive listening* is something you do from inside your head; it's more than just looking at them and pretending to be listening. Demonstrate how interested you are in what they are saying. Once you communicate an attitude of interest, your expressions, posture, and gestures will happily follow your mind.

Hint: One of the challenges of sitting through a venting session is that the topic is likely to be irrelevant to your life (and possibly uninteresting to you). Just how interested are you in the infighting going on during a planning meeting in a nuclear physics lab or at lunch in a preschool? Because the issues are so specific to the speaker, you're now confronting your own mental and emotional discord. You want this negative babble to stop, but you know you're going to be stuck here for a while. The question is: How long can you pretend you're interested? The answer is: You can't. So, get interested.

A person chooses someone they trust to listen to their upsets. This person may be a domestic partner, a friend, or a work colleague. Bottom line: They have placed their trust in you. You are responsible for living up to that trust—or don't agree to be their confidante in the first place. You repay that trust by being interested in what they're saying. It's as simple as that: Get interested or don't participate.

Don't be pushy

You may not be familiar with the setting about which the person is speaking; what they are saying may be confusing. When someone vents, they are releasing some of the negative emotion they have attached to an issue. The retelling can be skewed because the overall topic has an emotional (rather than purely logical) charge. This is not the time to try to make them see reason or minimize their feelings. Allow them to speak at their own pace, even if they explain their views in excruciating detail. You may be inclined to want to hurry them along to the conclusion. We suggest you not do that. Your patient listening and emotional support are most important at these times.

Communication effectiveness

Clear communication fosters good relationships. Obviously. While you probably can't sustain clear communication all the time, there are some steps you can take to tilt the odds in your favor. For example, you may create some stock phrases to use when you wish the conversation to go a certain way. Here are a few to get you started:

- "I'm going to vent now. Please don't give me advice."

- "I'm sharing an emotional experience; I would appreciate your empathy."

- "I am feeling angry about what has happened, and I suggest you leave me alone for the next X minutes or so."

- "We agreed to X and you have just done Y. I need your help understanding this."

- "We're just chatting. Let's just enjoy this and keep it lighthearted."

- "I need quiet time. Please don't speak to me until I signal you."

We have all been in situations where we thought we clearly understood someone, only to discover that we completely misunderstood
what the person meant. We weren't sure whether we misheard
them, or whether they were not clear. Here are some tips to help in
a few areas:

- Simplicity and directness

- Empathy and compassion

- Being in the moment

- Reading between the lines

Simplicity and directness

"Ah, just bring that stuff in here. Oh, and would you please run
to my toolbox and bring me my needle-nosed pliers and the roll of
black electrical tape? Oh, and my mallet."

Stuff? Needle-nosed pliers? Electrical tape? Mallet?

As we have asked: When you speak, do you use simple words, short
sentences, and clear word pictures? Here is a silly example I (Bob)
built one time to print and frame on my wall when I worked at the
Justice Department:

Original sentence   Research into the life expectancy of the variety of domesticated animals of the genus *Sus*,
commonly referred to as pigs, has shown that
the greatest threat to the possible decline of
this species has been engendered by the pred-
atorily inclined *Canis lupus*, often called wolf,
and its preferred diet of small mammals.

First revision   Research has shown that predatory wolves threaten the life expectancy of small pigs.

Final result   Wolves eat piglets.

Conclusion: *Keep it simple, silly.* Use as few words as you can; it keeps the communication clear. The easiest sentences to understand are short and use standard words. Don't obfuscate by using opaque syntax and esoteric argot. Be pellucid. (We are making a point by being playful.)

Empathy and compassion

In the heat of the moment, it is easy to forget that the person in front of you is not your enemy. *If only they could understand what I am trying to say! They must not be listening. They must not care about my feelings. In fact, it's obvious they really don't care about me!*

When we are frustrated and feeling unheard or misunderstood, it is a small step to feeling alone and unloved. When we feel such lonely and bitter emotions, it is easy to add our own spin about what the other person is feeling and thinking. The trouble is, we often react to *that* story rather than to what is really happening. The change from responding to what is actually being said to responding to the story you have created about what is being said is deadly. You have just stepped away from your logical brain into an emotional inferno.

Here is another challenge. As you react more and more to the tale you are telling yourself, the other person will rewrite their own story. Their narrative about why your responses are becoming more and more erratic and disproportionate to what is actually happening will skew their perspective. Now, you are both adrift in the sea of communication misalignment.

Remember: The other person probably feels many of the same vulnerable emotions in these heated moments. An argument can feel like a rejection of you as a person.

It has been our experience that upsets are better handled when we don't add our own dramatic translation of the other person's behavior. Our best suggestion is to approach the situation and the conversation with empathy and compassion for the other person. Hold on to the positive aspects of your partner(s), and most importantly, remember they are not the enemy. This practice helps keep the focus on the relevant issues. This technique stops us from permitting negative emotions or worst-case scenarios to cloud our perspective. It enables us to be more productive and focus on problem-solving as a team.

Slow down. Take the time to remove as many of these emotionally-charged filters (roadblocks) as possible. Listen in order to truly understand rather than merely to respond. Focus on communicating clearly and effectively. We will say it again: No one in this conversation is the enemy. Most people want positive outcomes so they can move on with a better understanding of the other person or people.

Look at these discussions as a way to strengthen your relationships. Even difficult conversations can be positive and healthy ways to get to know your partner(s) more deeply. Just like you, everyone is doing their very best in that moment to be heard and understood. A little empathy and compassion goes a long way towards leaving everyone feeling valued and validated.

We all listen with filters that translate what someone says into what we think they mean. Communication—when everyone feels safe and heard—leads to relationship harmony. Everyone feels able to share more deeply and honestly.

Being in the moment

Being in the moment is a complex ideal that can be difficult to attain. Holy people and gurus train their entire lives to get there. Let us explain it this way: When a moment passes, it's over. Once it's over, we are instantly in the next moment.

The question is: Are we fully engaged in this moment in time?

Here you are, now, in this moment, reading the words on this page. How much of what you are experiencing are you actually aware of? For example, are you aware of the room temperature? Are you aware of how comfortable or uncomfortable you feel in the position you're in? Are there parts of your body that are communicating with you that you are not hearing because you are not present in this moment?

While physically in the present, we often think about our past with regret and our future with fear. This can occur when we drag past experiences with us; they can become our constant companions. We are further distanced from being in the moment as our reactive brains project our past experiences into our imagined (chaotic) future. We are challenged to live in the present, to the extent we dwell in that fear.

This situation applies to all people at all times. When it comes to communication, we offer you these questions: Are both the speaker and the listener truly *present* for the conversation? Are they listening with intent, or is their mind drifting elsewhere? Are they speaking from the present, or are they listening with an overlay comprised of past issues and future fears?

How do you convey to the other person that you are actively engaged in the conversation? The two of you may want to work out signals that mean, essentially, *I have something to say; please listen actively.*

The new question is: Are you communicating your attentiveness?

- When sitting, sit forward.

- Maintain eye contact.

- Ensure your replies support the conversation.

- Repeat what you think you heard. Demonstrate active listening.

- Nod or shake your head at appropriate times.

- Speak with full thoughts. Use simple words.

- Double-check that your listener has understood your message before moving on to the next point.

When we are not in the present, we tend to fall into automatic sub-routines that require little attention. When there is a lack of new, usable, or relevant content in a conversation, some people may tune out. They stop *hearing* you. Think about your evening conversations. Your partner has arrived home from work. You ask about their day, as you do every evening when they come home from work. You don't really expect any response beyond *fine* or *good* or *okay*. You're not really listening and they're not really talking. After all, your story is basically the same day after day. No personal insights; no fresh adventures; no new ideas. Your partner may wonder why you are even asking.

Routine (or almost rote) conversation can be a sign that someone is phoning it in, as it were. They are not putting in much effort. However, remember this: If you're not *working* on your relationship, you're not really *in* a relationship.

There are many reasons in-the-moment presence can be hard for a person. One challenge is to develop the skill to quiet your own

background noise and listen to the speaker with focus. You can practice this by listening to the news on the radio. See how long you can
listen to the broadcast without your mind refocusing to some personal thoughts. You'll be surprised how difficult this can be.

> Being present can mean extending an effort in each moment to
> be the best listener (receiver) and communicator (transmitter)
> possible to show *this* conversation matters.

In face-to-face (or even telephone) conversations, such attentiveness
shows honor and respect towards both the speaker and the listener—
always a good thing.

Reading between the lines

"I am going to run to the store for a second. When I get home, this
house had better be sparkling from top to bottom or I am going to
mop the floor with you."

"Oh yeah? Who died and left you commander-in-chief? Go jump
in the lake!"

What do you make of that paragraph? Is this exchange threatening?
Silly? Friendly? You can read that paragraph as two people who are
playing around or about to erupt into domestic violence. You need
more information in order to make sense from what these two people are meaning. You derive meaning from:

- Tone

- Inflection

- Facial expression

- Volume

- Historical context

When we speak, most of us are trying to be as clear as possible. This is doubly true for important conversations. This part of the book is tricky because we are discussing more than simply words and word use. We are discussing *intention* and *nuance*. This is the area where *how you say something* can change *what you communicate*.

As you grow up, you become better at recognizing and translating things such as sarcasm, dry wit, and deadpan humor. The sense and connotation of English words or sentences can change dramatically just by the inflection they are given. However, in our modern English, such nuance is lost when writing and reading texts or emails.

Here are a few quick examples of how sentence meaning changes as a result of stressing (or inflecting) certain words:

- "Please close the door." Spoken evenly and with no inflection. This is what you would generally expect for a first request.

- "Please... close the door." All the words are evenly emphasized, but the added pause makes the phrase into an invitation. It affirms it is okay for you to close the door.

- "**Please** close the door." This is emphatic. It is important to the speaker that you close the door *now*.

- "Please **close** the door." Said with feeling. Don't just leave it ajar; *shut it.*

- "Please close the **door**." Evidently there was some confusion about what the speaker wanted closed or there was an obvious choice between *door* and something else.

Again, this is why email and text messages can so often be misinterpreted. Clearly, good communication does not rest simply in *what* you say. It rests in *how* you say it, *where* you say it, *when* you say it, and *with whom* you are speaking.

Defense mechanisms

Speaking and listening can be tremendously affected by things having nothing to do with the actual conversation. For example, how we feel about someone influences how we receive and transmit information. Speaking personally, I (Bob) think that these issues have given me more trouble over the years than any other aspect of communication.

In psychology, *displacement* refers to the unconscious defense mechanism that redirects feelings about one person onto another person. For instance, you might mistrust somebody who shares some of an ex-partner's mannerisms, voice, or physical looks. Or you may feel comfortable around someone who resembles one of your parents.

Psychological *projection* (or projection bias) is the term used to describe an ego defense mechanism wherein you attribute (or *project*) your own unacceptable or unwanted thoughts or emotions to another person. This occurs because you dislike some aspect of your own behavior, and when you see someone else exhibiting similar behavior, you react negatively to that person even though they have not done anything to demonstrate unworthiness or untrustworthiness.

For example, projection may occur in a current domestic relationship when someone cheated on an ex in the past. They may be very possessive and mistrust a new partner's fidelity. This mistrust is based on projecting *their own prior behavior* onto their partner who, in fact, was just working late one evening. That is, a person projects their own insecurities or weaknesses onto another person and then reacts to those projections as though they are real.

It doesn't take a rocket scientist to realize that once one person starts reacting to their own projected insecurities, the relationship has headed down a path filled with misunderstandings and hurt feelings.

If one partner's projections go unchecked, both partners will increasingly grow wary of one another. One partner is seeing dragons under the bed while the other partner cannot figure out what they did to trigger this negative pattern.

The highest cliff you can fall from is trust.

COLLAPSE AND MARK TWAIN

There is a Landmark Education Forum article titled "A Portal to the Domain of Possibility" by Jane Wright. Here it is with minor edits.

Something happens.

We instantly assign meaning to it. We evaluate its importance and draw conclusions. In some ways, our version of the event differs from what objectively happened. Our version can be said to have *collapsed* upon what *really* happened. From this point on, our version of the event **is** the event.

This collapse between what happened and the meanings we assign to it takes place instantly. We aren't aware of any distinction between what actually happened and what we made it mean to us. As they often point out in The Landmark Education Forum, these two things—what happened and what you remember—are two independent and totally separate occurrences.

This is where Mark Twain comes in. Famously, he authored this bit of insight: "It's not what you don't know that gets you in trouble. It's what you know for sure that just ain't so."

Chapter 6
Communication styles and suggestions

SUCCESSFUL COMMUNICATION IS COMPLICATED. There is no magic pill. You, just being you, adds complexities (filters) that include your age, gender, background, and life experiences.

This section is intended to expose you to some ways of thinking about communication. You may be familiar with some of these; others may surprise you:

- Processing modalities

- Love languages

- Ego states

- The importance of words

Processing modalities

As humans, we depend upon our senses (touch, taste, smell, hearing, sight) to give us a composite picture of our everyday reality. We have no way to evaluate the physical world beyond our sensory channels. Our interpretation of the world becomes our reality. Our reality, then, is a combination of what our senses transmit back to us.

Blended together, these senses create our unique frame of reality. No one else experiences reality in exactly the same way we do. Over time—from infancy to adulthood—we gradually develop a preference for one or two of our senses.

In your daily life, your behaviors signal your sensory preferences. For example, if you are highly visual, you probably like your home to look a certain way; neatness may matter more than cleanliness. Similarly, if you are tactile, you might choose clothing based on how it feels and prefer sleeping on high thread-count sheets. Selecting audiobooks (instead of printed words) might indicate you are auditory. Needing to see things written down before fully comprehending the material might signal that you are visual. A good way to tell how you like to process information is by how you remember the past. Someone who has an olfactory preference might remember past events by smell.

This is relevant, because communication effectiveness is improved by building rapport. To build rapport, it helps to know how you and others with whom you communicate take in information.

While rapport is important, it is not helpful in every situation. There are times when rapport can actually decrease effective communication. For example, there are many times when we simply need to deliver a message; we're not interested in emotional connection. If you need to notify your co-worker that your boss wants a report on their desk by Thursday, you may not need to start by establishing rapport. It probably isn't necessary to first ask how their day is going, hear about their health, and look at pictures of their children and grandchildren. The issue is the report deadline, nothing more.

When communication benefits from establishing a sense of connection or familiarity with the other person, the more you know about ways to build rapport, the better. A good way to quickly and effectively establish rapport with someone new is to identify and mirror their reality-processing preferences. For example, if you know they process information visually, using visual language (such as *I see* or *That's a good view*) will make them (subconsciously) sense you are easy to speak with.

You can increase the value of gifts you give by recognizing the other person's processing modalities. Otherwise, mismatches in processing modalities can complicate even the simple act of gift giving. For example, if a high-visual person gives the gift of a painting to a high-auditory person, the gift may not be received with as much meaning as the giver had intended. To a tactile person, a gift of high thread-count sheets would be appreciated more than it would be by a person who takes in information by smell.

Some gifts cross processing preferences. For example, flowers will be appreciated both by those who are high-visual and high-olfactory.

Here is a quick review of the five principal ways people take in information from the world around them. As you see, they reflect the five senses and represent some of the different ways you may wish to adjust the way you express yourself to meet your listener's preferences. This helps the other person better understand what you're talking about.

- **Auditory.** The speaker uses phrases such as *I hear you, That sounds good to me,* or *You can say that again.*

- **Visual.** The speaker uses phrases such as *I see what you mean* or *It looks like a problem.*

- **Kinesthetic.** The speaker uses phrases such as *That feels right to me, I'm comfortable with that,* or *I'm touched by that story.*

- **Gustatory.** The speaker uses phrases such as *That outfit is yummy*, *This leaves a bad taste in my mouth*, or *Isn't this event delicious?*

- **Olfactory.** The speaker uses phrases such as *This deal smells fishy to me* or *This entire situation stinks.*

When you hear these cues, you can readjust your language to mirror this person's information processing preferences.

Love languages

Do you know how to communicate your love to your partner in a way that they understand and feel? Do you know how to communicate respect or admiration to a co-worker in a way that they will recognize and appreciate? We assert that it is important to know how *love languages* can be used both at home and at work.

In his book (*The Five Love Languages: The Secret to Love that Lasts*), Gary Chapman lists the common ways people communicate love. It's a good resource. Chapman explains how to recognize and appreciate acts of love, even if they aren't something you would normally associate with your concept of love. The overall conclusion is that it's important to know how you want love expressed to you and it's important that your partner knows about their own language of love. Obviously, this topic is worth a good sit-down discussion.

Often referenced, these are Chapman's five love languages:

1   **Money/gifts.** Some people give money or gifts to say *I love you*. They consider the act of giving to be a complete demonstration of love. For example, they may turn over their paycheck to their partner or routinely provide small tokens of their affection.

2   **Physical touch.** Some people use touch to say *I love you.* They thrive on constant physical affections. For example, they may stroke their partner's hand in the car or provide back and foot massages in the evenings.

3   **Performing services.** Some people perform acts of service to say *I love you.* They take pride in doing something for their partner before the other person even thinks of doing it for themselves. For example, they may have a steaming cup of perfectly pre-pared coffee ready each morning before their partner has even made it to the kitchen.

4   **Time and attention.** Some people spend quality time with their partner to say *I love you.* They consider the amount of time spent with the other person to be an indicator of the depth of their love. For example, they may enjoy date nights or quality time together away from distractions such as television and other people.

5   **Verbal.** Some people use words to say *I love you.* They connect emotionally with what they say and what is said to them. For example, they may frequently use verbal affirmations, such as *Good job, Nice work, I really appreciate it when you...*

Obviously, it's important that both partners feel accepted for the lan-guage of love they bring to the relationship, and also that they are genuinely able to accept their partner's language of love. The thing of it is, there are lots of missed opportunities both with couples and co-workers. This happens when one person's message goes unrec-ognized by the other person. This is seldom a deliberate act; it's an invisibility issue. *Let's go out for dinner* may really mean, *Tell me you love me by spending time with me.*

The possibilities for missing the mark are endless. However, with improved communication, the possibilities of success are spectacular.

Once you are both aware of different kinds of love languages, you can begin to spot and acknowledge acts of love from the other's viewpoint (even though such acts may not meet your own particular needs). As you can imagine, it is important that you and your partner explore and define what makes each of you feel loved.

It's wonderful when partners have the same love languages, as they can easily see and appreciate the other's efforts. However, when love languages differ, both partners will need to:

- Acknowledge the other's expressions of love, even if it isn't particularly meaningful to you

- Attempt to communicate love in the language that is more easily understood and appreciated by your partner

- Discuss individual preferences with your partner so that the other person knows what you want. (Don't make them guess and then find fault with them for not guessing correctly.)

The skill of identifying other people's love language applies beyond personal relationships. For example, let's say one of your co-workers is a great team member. As someone whose love language is *gift giving*, your usual way of thanking a team member is to give a Starbucks gift card. However, you've determined that their love language is *words of affirmation*. Taking advantage of your knowledge, you decide against the gift card and rally the entire team to verbally express a heartfelt *Thank you*.

If you wish to explore this topic in more depth, we urge you to take a look at some NLP (neuro-linguistic programming) material. We each have studied NLP for over a decade and believe it has vastly improved our interpersonal and communication skills.

Learn to communicate in all the languages of love and learn to recognize and value the ways others convey their love for you. Oh, and be sensitive to your partner's strengths and weaknesses. Play to strengths; it builds your relationship. Support each other's weaknesses; it builds trust.

Ego states

It can be complicated to work through conflicts, particularly when volatile emotions are involved. De-escalation begins with understanding whether or not you are even on the same emotional page. Fortunately, a field of study called *transactional analysis* (TA) emerged from the study of communication upsets. TA views each part of a conversation as a transaction. The transaction is phrased in one of three ways: as an adult, as a parent, or as a child.

Because this is such an important aspect of successful communication, we will take some time to go over it.

All quoted material in this section comes from the writings of Alan Chapman (<u>businessballs.com</u>). We can't improve on his writing.

According to Chapman, the psychiatrist Eric Berne formulated the concept of transactional analysis in the 1950s. He observed that personal relationships involve one person speaking with another person. TA is focused on understanding how and why verbal communication between two people succeed or fail. (TA won't apply to texts or email, because word inflection carries meaning in spoken English, and you need to be able to interpret word inflection to perform this analysis.)

Berne was able to pinpoint three *alter-ego states* that exist to one degree or another in every person:

1   **Parent ego state.** In "psychology speak," the *parent* voice has the ring of authority. It reflects absorbed cultural conditioning. When confronted with a situation that goes against your learned beliefs, you hear your parent voice reaffirming what you were taught as a child. You will then assert reactions based on your (possibly) flawed assumptions about the world around you. For example, image that you and a friend are walking into a subway station. They suggest jumping over the turnstile to avoid paying the fare. Instantly, you hear a parental voice telling you that doing so is stealing and only bad people steal. If you did this, you too are a bad person. So you react by saying "We can't do that! That is wrong."

The phrase *We can't do that!* is expressed as your parent voice, full of instructions and judgments about what you (or someone else) should or shouldn't do. Often, when you express wall or limits about something you believe to be true, you are speaking in parent voice. Watch for words that are absolutes such as: can't, won't, must, always, never, etc.

The parent ego state is a collection of prerecorded codes of conduct. It expresses itself as a hardwired collection of prejudged standards for life. This is the voice that automatically decides how to react to situations. It knows ahead of time what is good or bad. It has already decided how people should live. The parent voice judges for or against almost everything based on opinion rather than fact.

2   **Child ego state.** When we are in our *child* ego state, we react emotionally to the world around us. Think back on the behaviors of small children. When overcome with feelings, they often react in ways that exacerbate (rather than logically resolve) a situation. More than that, emotional reactions learned as a child can manifest as an adult (often to your surprise). For example,

let us imagine that your parents called you lazy or messy as a child. Now, fully grown and married, your spouse returns from work one day and casually comments that the house is a mess. You might *react* emotionally rather than *assess* and *respond neutrally*. This reaction may be a sign that your inner child has taken over. You may explode with hurt or anger, or perhaps withdraw emotionally.

Your lingering child voice is powerful. It is emotion-driven and self-centered. It also resists the self-regulation that comes with adulthood. It can be difficult to overcome emotional reactions to deep-seated landmines that trigger child voice.

3   **Adult ego state.** Our *adult* persona represents our capability to think and to act independently, based on correctly decoding and interpreting what is happening around us. From a young age, children begin to learn lessons that will ultimately form their adult ego state. To remain present in our adult ego state, it helps to understand (and gain control over) our parent and child ego states.

All three ego states combine to make up a whole person's personality. To summarize:

- Your parent voice projects what you've been *taught* to understand about life. You tend to use this voice when explaining something to someone, particularly a subordinate.

- Your child voice projects how you *feel* about life. This voice comes out when your feelings are hurt—or when you are pressured to complete a project and are tired.

- Your adult voice projects how you've come to *think* about life. It's what you say when you speak to yourself.

As we go through this material, you will realize that adult-to-adult communication holds the key to stabilizing everyday conversations.

You may wonder why we are going into this level of detail about TA. The answer is that we all communicate from one or another of our own ego states—*parent, child,* or *adult.* The situation—and our own frame of mind—determines which persona will do the talking. Moreover, something can trigger an unconscious and instantaneous shift from one state to another and back again, without missing a beat.

Berne's great discovery was that successful communication must be **complementary.** The response should be from the same ego state as the initial communication or it is said to be *crossed.* Crossed communication often triggers a communication breakdown. The real message isn't completely received. Unfortunately, neither person may realize that something was missed.

In the ideal communication model, both parties speak from their adult ego states. If you find yourself involved in a conversation that isn't going as expected, you may want to stop and assess which ego states each of you are using. That is, are either of you speaking from your parent or child ego states?

If the person with whom you are speaking is reacting from their parent or child ego state, your challenge is to learn how to move the conversation away from the land of emotions or judgment and back to stability by first reflecting their ego state and then replying from your adult ego state.

Note: If someone is speaking in parent voice, they are speaking as if their opinions are truths. While you may not entirely agree, you can usually find some common ground that enables you to begin to defuse the conversation and move into adult voice.

Here's an example of how someone making a statement in *parent voice* may be neutralized by responding in *adult voice*:

Statement	(parent voice) "I can't believe you were late to the meeting! That shows you have absolutely no respect for other people's time!"
First response	(parent voice) "Oh gosh, it is disrespectful to be late!"
Second response	(adult voice) "You are correct. Being on time isn't really good enough, I need to be early."

Speaking in adult voice generally defuses the situation and enables the conversation to continue smoothly.

Here's an example of how to respond to *child voice*:

Statement	(child voice) "What do you mean I need to turn in my report by tomorrow! Our boss never gives us enough notice; she sucks. I don't feel like doing it!"
First response	(child voice) "Short notice does suck! I don't like rushing either."
Second response	(adult voice) "You know, now that I'm thinking about this, how about if we work this out together. Maybe I can help you."

If your goal is to *defuse* the situation, respond with empathy. If your desire is to *resolve* the situation, move into adult voice and create space for them to do the same.

Here's an example of how crossed communication might unfold:

Person A   (adult voice) "This personal project we're doing is going so well, I'm really pumped. I just finished the part I promised you. How is your section coming along?"

Person B   (child voice) "I can't believe you asked me that right now! You must think I'm made of energy. I've had such a bad day, which I would have told you if you'd asked me about it. Now I'm in a really bad mood. I don't want to do anything at the moment."

Person A   (parent voice) "Now listen, you know I can't start the next section until you're done with yours. In order for us to be a good team, you need to finish your portion."

Person B   (child voice) "I can't stand it when you speak to me that way. Do you really expect me to stay up and finish this? I'll be tired at work tomorrow. Maybe I should just call in."

Person A   (parent voice) "Calling in when you aren't ill is dishonest. I just need you to get it done."

Although this exchange started with a neutral adult-voice question, when Person B reacted from their child ego state, it triggered Person A's emotional response, causing them to reply from their own parent ego state. Once this happened, the two of them became locked in a parent–child, emotion-filled loop. At the end of this short exchange, it is evident that Person A actually missed Person B's underlying message: *I'm burned out. I need a break and your emotional support.*

The exchange would have proceeded more smoothly if Person A's initial reaction had also been from their child (rather than parent) ego state. For example, they could have countered with: "You had a bad day. Gosh, that sucks! I don't want to do anything after I've had a bad day, either."

Once Person A has validated and expressed compassion, they can now attempt to create a safe space that encourages Person B to continue the conversation in adult voice. An example:

Person B   "Yes, that's right. I don't want to have to think after a bad day at work. I'm glad you understand."

Person A   "How about I run you a bath and we relax and watch a movie—unless you're ready to go to bed. We don't have to talk about this now. A day off will only make us more productive, anyway."

Person B   "Thanks for understanding. I really need the evening off. I know I'll feel more like working on this tomorrow."

We have introduced you to TA to help you identify how crossed communication can derail a conversation. Once you realize the signs (and change your own speaking patterns), you will be better equipped to start looking for the intended message.

Remember, we began this section by explaining that effective communication is complementary. It happens when you are both speaking from the same ego state. Crossed communication (when the speaker and respondent are speaking from different ego states) can trigger reactiveness and resistance; your best shot for stabilizing a derailed conversation is to respond to your communication partner from *their* ego state before trying to pull both of you into an adult voice. Generally speaking, adult-to-adult conversations are the most stable and productive means of communication.

The communication deck is stacked steeply against you. However, TA reveals a magic formula that simplifies communication complexity. As you understand and practice the lessons offered by considering each exchange of words in a conversation as a transaction, you will realize that you now have the power to consistently create high-quality adult-to-adult conversations. This is a game changer. You now have the power to help move someone from child or parent ego state to adult ego state. You now have the power to reduce the drama in conversations.

Ultimately, improving your communication skills improves your relationships, both at work and at home. That's a happy byproduct of effective communication.

The importance of words

A Thai monk, Achann Chaa of Wat Po Pong, is credited with having said:

> Watch your thoughts, they become words.
> Watch your words, they become actions.
> Watch your actions, they become habits.
> Watch your habits, they become character.
> Watch your character, it becomes your destiny.

Word choice strongly influences your ability to communicate complex ideas and steer a conversation toward or away from crisis. Most critically, word choice holds the key to speaking from your adult ego state.

It matters whether you create sentences that project a positive or negative outlook. *I have to take care of the kids all day* sends a different message than, *I get to spend time with my children today.*

When you are speaking with someone, it matters whether you choose words that are easy to understand or challenging. It matters whether your intent is to transfer information, to convince someone of something, or to be right. Are your words describing facts, possibilities, or fears?

Word choice is important. If you already use positive words, this section will reinforce that.

The way you *name* things can affect many aspects of your relationships both at work and at home. How you perceive and name events also strongly influences your outlook on life.

Our general perspective about whether our world and our experiences are positive or negative deeply affects our resiliency. It can also affect whether we are willing and able to take responsibility for ourselves. As an example, if you see something as a problem rather than as an opportunity, you're partly handicapped from the outset by having a negative perspective. If you live in a world of absolutes (*always, never, can't*, etc.), it may not occur to you that there actually are options. As you are in charge of yourself, you are also in charge of the words you pick to color events and the world around you.

Here are a few examples of words that can help move you into a more positive frame of mind:

- **Change *problems* to *opportunities*.** Speaking negatively, you might say to your partner, "I think we have a problem here." From your perspective, this might be both true and accurate; you have a problem that needs to be resolved and fixed.

  In English, *problems* tend to stump people; they are a puzzle. Often, they carry a negative connotation and imply failure or defeat. Similarly, *mistakes* imply an absence or lack of success. I (Veronica) don't subscribe to that definition. Personally, my greatest growth occurs when my life doesn't go according to plan.

For example, was it a mistake to *finally* say **Yes!** to my beloved—days before we discovered he had stage IV cancer? No, though some might disagree. Were there lots of problems and issues? Absolutely, if you want to look at it that way. But, because of our shared outlook on life, we saw problems as opportunities to love harder and live each moment together as though it were our last. We crammed a lifetime of living into two short years. Rather than a mistake, our time together has become my touchstone for joy and hope. I consider those two years (and the lessons that came from that time) to be his perpetual gift.

Translation: Use a positive construction, such as, *Okay, this didn't work. What can we learn from it?* to lead you to seek opportunities for new knowledge, more growth, and better future results. Positive framing helps avoid negative emotional loading. Better yet, *opportunities* tend to be viewed as gifts. With a positive perspective, you can look at mistakes as speed bumps rather than stop signs and develop a resilience to adversity.

• **Absolutely never use absolutes.** Words that express extreme positions (such as *always* and *never*) pack an emotional punch. Saying "You always get the job done!" can make a co-worker feel like a superhero at work or add undue pressure that they must always perform to that standard. Just as effectively, "You never get the job done!" can trigger feelings of inadequacy and poor self-worth.

Interestingly, extreme words such as *never* and *always* are never true (that's a joke). Okay, they are seldom true.

Sure, you can say, *The sun always comes up from the east.* But that is a scientific comment, not an opinion you are sharing with someone. In the soft sciences, very little is absolute. Moreover, extreme words often exaggerate a situation and also reveal quite a bit about your own emotional loading about the subject being discussed. When someone is swept up in emotion, they frequently start using phrasing such as, *You are always mad*, *You are never happy*, and *I can't ever please you*. The person receiving these absolutes may miss or ignore the intended message and instead become defensive or withdrawn. It may help to remember that speaking in absolutes might be a cry for attention or help. It may also be that they are lashing out as a defense mechanism.

As an alternative to using *absolutes* in your communications, we recommend phrasing we have already mentioned: *When you said x, I made that mean y.* This approach holds you accountable for how you perceived that action in light of your personal filters. This approach also minimizes the chance that what you say will invoke the other person's defensiveness. Now, you are much more likely to resolve the upset peacefully and quickly.

- **Turn *shoulds* into *coulds*.** A negative statement (in parent voice) could be, "You should exercise every day and try to stay in shape." An alternate (and more positive version in adult voice) could be, "Our health is important. Could we work together on an exercise routine we could do as a couple?"

The first construction shifts blame (or responsibility) onto the other person and sets up feelings such as anger, guilt, and shame for not behaving as they had been told. By recasting the request as a positive joint project avoids the negative spin.

- **Make *faults* into *differences*.** "It's your fault you can't find anything in your closet: Your closet is a total mess as usual!" Contrast this with, "You seemed upset last night that you couldn't find what you were looking for in your closet. I organize my closet a little differently now because I've had similar issues myself. Would you like me to help you work on it?"

If you use the word *fault*, you are judging someone (or their actions) as wrong. They are likely to become defensive and resent what you're trying to say to them. Using the word *different* removes the critical tone and does not imply one of you is better than the other. You're simply pointing out how the two of you process, feel, or act differently.

The bottom line is that words can be either destructive or constructive. They can tear down or enrich your relationships—whether we are speaking about your relationships with your partner or with your co-workers.

Now for the hard part. To accomplish this transformation, you need to think before you speak. Your everyday happiness depends upon it. Many of us get stuck with wanting to be right. As a consequence, we tend to hold our ground in discussions beyond the point where it is good for the relationship. This has given rise to the quip: Which would you rather be, *right* or *happy*?

Our closing thoughts

- Relationships that are consciously chosen are usually more rewarding than relationships built on default assumptions.

- Relationships are often different in theory than in practice.

- Being in a relationship that does not meet your needs is not necessarily better than being alone.

- Remember: You're supposed to be having fun, that's why you got together (or took this job) in the first place.

Ah, and here is an acronym to take with you...

When all else fails, remember LOVE:

- **L**isten to understand

- **O**ffer information rather than try to prove a point

- **V**alidate and accept the other person's feelings

- **E**nd on a positive note

Well, it's safe now to unfasten your seatbelt. We have reached our destination. We hope you have enjoyed the journey. We certainly thank you for the steadfastness it took to work through this book and make it to this page.

As we have repeatedly emphasized, you are responsible for listening to understand rather than listening to respond. You are in the driver's seat and can use your skills to guide conversations to mutually beneficial conclusions.

This book has provided a wide range of insights and options intended to give you practical ideas to build communication skills that work for you. We have covered a lot of material, and we hope this book will continue to serve as a touchstone that you can return to repeatedly to discover or refresh useful techniques.

We always enjoy meeting our readers, so please feel free to come up and say hello if you find yourself at a conference with us.

—Robert (Bob) Rubel and Veronica Petterson

Supplementary material

Preparing for normal accidents

Basic information

On your cell phone, download an ICE (in case of emergency) app and fill it out with required information.

In your home and/or wallet/purse, keep lists in an easy-to-find location with information including:

- Phone numbers for your employer, close friends, and/or family members (plus the calling order)

- Medications and dosage with the name and phone number of the prescribing doctor

- Instructions and details in the event that you are incapacitated

Legal documents

Store your legal documents where they can be found easily. These include your:

- Will

- Medical POAs (powers of attorney), covering when (or whether or not) the doctor/hospital is to use:

  - Resuscitation

  - Heroic measures to save your life

  - Mechanical ventilation

  - Tube feeding

  - Dialysis

  - Antibiotics or antiviral medications

  - Comfort care (palliative care)

  - Organ and tissue donations

  Note: These should also be on file with your doctor.

- Financial and other POAs (if applicable)

By the way, you're never too young to have a will. Not only should you have one, but you should also be reviewing it every five years or so.

Digital details

Consider all the things you do online to ensure your life runs smoothly. You might the pay bills, pay the rent or mortgage, monitor your bank accounts, or manage your assets and investments.

In the event that you are incapacitated, can your partner continue overseeing these day-to-day necessities for the both of you? Perhaps you live together, but don't have joint bank accounts. Or, only one of you is listed on the lease or mortgage. Or, they don't know which bills need to be paid and when.

It can be very difficult to get access to your online accounts if your partner doesn't know the URLs, usernames, and passwords in advance. There is a number of ways to manage this, but the most private and secure one is to pay a couple dollars a month on a password manager called LastPass (lastpass.com). This service saves (and encrypts) all your myriad usernames and passwords, such that you can log into these accounts with a single *master password*.

More importantly, it allows you to designate an emergency contact. This person can request access to your account. In the case that you are unable to respond, and after a designated period of time has elapsed, they are automatically granted permission. You can even add informational or instructional notes for this person and associate them with specific credentials.

Other considerations

Here are a few other things to think about when it comes to preparing for emergencies:

- Are bank accounts joint, so that if one partner is hospitalized the surviving partner can pay current bills?

- Do you keep cash or valuables at your house? If so, where are they?

- Where will the remaining partner live if something happens to the other? Who is listed on the lease or mortgage?

- What happens if one partner is incapacitated long-term but doesn't die? Do you have insurance that covers this? Do you have savings to cover basic expenses for a few months?

- If you have outside investments, what are they and what would someone need to know about them if you are incapacitated for a time?

Cited works

Chapter 1

- The 7 Habits of Highly Effective People: Powerful Lessons in Personal Change (25th Anniversary Edition) by Stephen R. Covey

- A Russell Hoban Omnibus by Russell Hoban

- The Crack in the Cosmic Egg: New Constructs of Mind and Reality (Revised Edition) by Joseph Chilton Pearce

- How to Give and Receive Advice by Gerard L. Nierenberg

- Nonviolent Communication: A Language of Life (Third Edition) by Marshall B. Rosenberg

- What To Say When You Talk to Yourself by Shad Helmstetter

Chapter 2

- Outliers: The Story of Success by Malcolm Gladwell

- Crucial Conversations: Tools for Talking When Stakes Are High (Second Edition) by Kerry Patterson, Joseph Grenny, Ron McMillan, and Al Switzler

- The Order of Time by Carlo Rovelli

- Time and Intimacy: A New Science of Personal Relationships by Joel B. Bennett

- Unlimited Power: The New Science of Personal Achievement by Anthony Robbins

- Relationship Principles by Franklin Veaux. tacit.livejournal. com/388290.html

Chapter 3

- **The Usual Error: Why We Don't Understand Each Other and 34 Ways to Make It Better** by Pace Smith and Kyeli Smith

- **Lateral Thinking: Creativity Step by Step** by Edward DeBono

- **Thinking Better: A Revolutionary New Program to Achieve Peak Mental Performance** by David Lewis and James Greene

- **The Ideal Problem Solver: A Guide to Improving Thinking, Learning, and Creativity** by John D. Bransford and Barry S. Stein

- **Teaching Thinking Skills: Theory and Practice** by Joan Boykoff Baron and Robert J. Sternberg

- **The Art of Thinking: The Classic Guide to Increasing Brain Power** by Allen F. Harrison and Robert M. Bramson

- **Feeling Good: The New Mood Therapy** (Reprint Edition) by David D. Burns

- **Gifts Differing: Understanding Personality Type** by Isabel Briggs Myers with Peter B. Myers

- **Please Understand Me: Character and Temperament Types** by David Keirsey and Marilyn Bates

- **Please Understand Me II: Temperament Character Intelligence** by David Keirsey. **Type Talk at Work: How the Sixteen Personality Types Determine Your Success on the Job** by Otto Groeger with Janet M. Thuesen and Hile Rutledge

- **Understanding the Mysteries of Human Behavior** by Mark Leary. The Great Courses

- **The Five Languages of Apology: How to Experience Healing in All Your Relationships** by Gary Chapman and Jennifer Thomas

- Red Flags by Saikiji Kitalpha. facebook.com/learningkink/posts/learningtime-dominant-vs-domineering-relationship-red-flag-listposted-on-january/1031113900367420 (repost)

Chapter 4

- Emotional Intelligence: Why It Can Matter More Than IQ by Daniel Goleman

- EQ Applied: The Real-World Guide to Emotional Intelligence by Justin Bariso

- Never Be Lied to Again: How to Get the Truth in 5 Minutes or Less in Any Conversation or Situation by David J. Lieberman

- What Every BODY is Saying: An Ex-FBI Agent's Guide to Speed-Reading People by Joe Navarro with Marvin Karlins

- Read 'Em and Reap: A Career FBI Agent's Guide to Decoding Poker Tells by Joe Navarro with Marvin Karlins

- Liespotting: Proven Techniques to Detect Deception by Pamela Meyer

Chapter 5

- Bridges Not Walls: A Book About Interpersonal Communication by John Stewart

- Words that Sell: More than 6000 Entries to Help You Promote Your Products, Services, and Ideas by Richard Bayan

- The Importance of Neutral Questions by Charles MacInerney. selfgrowth.com/articles/The_Importance_Of_Neutral_Questions.html

- **The Right Mountain: Lessons from Everest on the Real Meaning of Success** by Jim Hayhurst Sr.

- **MindWorks: A Practical Guide for Changing Thoughts, Beliefs and Emotional Reactions** by Gary van Warmerdam

- **Simple Tips on Having the Hard Conversation** by John Rydell. web.archive.org/web/20160313010157/http://entrepreneursun-pluggd.com/blog/simple-tips-on-having-the-hard-conversation

- **Men Are from Mars, Women Are from Venus** by John Gray

- **Flightdeck Performance: The Human Factor** by David O'Hare

Chapter 6

- **A Portal to the Domain of Possibility** by Jane Wright. landmar-kinsights.com/2012/10/a-portal-to-the-domain-of-possibility

- **The Five Love Languages: The Secret to Love that Lasts** (Reprint Edition) by Gary Chapman

Acknowledgments

We particularly recognize Patrick Califia for his exemplary work editing our book. You certainly have raised it to a much higher level than when you received it.

We also thank kitara for preparing this book for publication. I (Veronica) believe this is the seventh book she has done for Bob. Clearly, we are delighted!

I (Bob) also wish to thank Renee St. James for being my Patron for the past many years. It's odd to think of it that way, but that is the reality of it. I simply could not produce these books without her continued support.

Thank you.

About the authors

Robert J. Rubel, PhD

Dr. Rubel is an educational sociologist and researcher by training and an author, lecturer, and photographer by choice. Since 2006, he has written over a dozen books, mostly on communications and relationship issues. Dr. Rubel has lost count of the number of conferences, clubs, and weekend intensives he has presented. At 76, he continues to present world-wide about 5–8 times a year—now virtually, due to the pandemic.

Veronica Petterson

Veronica Petterson is a professional life coach, relationship counselor, and relationship workshop facilitator. Since 2001, she has presented classes on topics such as relationships, communication, radical transformation, dealing with grief, and female empowerment. A former radio talk show host, she is best known for her educational efforts and advocacy for strong (yet vulnerable) women in sustainable leadership. She divides her time between volunteering in her community, investing in real estate, recruiting/training for her real estate brokerage firm (director of agency development), and helping clients buy and sell their property.